A Guide to Collecting

Silver

ELIZABETH DE CASTRES

Published in association with
J. GODDARD AND SONS LTD

BLOOMSBURY BOOKS

© Elizabeth de Castres/J. Goddard and Sons Limited 1980

Designed by Janet James

Front cover: teapot and stand by Daniel Denny, London, 1800 (photograph: Tony Latham, teapot: John Laurie Antiques Ltd)

Back cover: soup tureen and ladle by Christopher Dresser for Hukin and Heath, 1880 (Cooper-Bridgeman Library/Ian Bennett Collection)

Previous page: tea kettle and stand by Paul de Lamerie, London, 1732 (Christie's)

For Timothy

ISBN 0 906223 67 9

First published in 1980 by Queen Anne Press, Macdonald Futura Publishers.

This edition 1985 published by
Bloomsbury Books
an imprint of Godfrey Cave Associates Ltd
42 Bloomsbury Street, London WC1B 3QJ

Printed and bound in Yugoslavia by
Mladinska Knjiga, Ljubljana

Contents

Foreword

I am delighted that Goddard's are associated with a book that not only nurtures the tremendous growth of interest in silver which we have seen in recent years, but also gives practical advice on how to start a collection and care for it too. The variety of items which have been wrought in silver over the centuries is boundless, and I am sure you will find great pleasure in starting even the smallest and simplest collection of your own.

Historically, my family has been closely connected with silver and its care for over 140 years. My great-grandfather, Joseph Goddard, developed the original Non-Mercurial Plate Powder, which was the first proprietary silver polish in the world, and became the forerunner of a complete range of products that now solves every type of silver cleaning problem.

This fascinating book will, I am sure, give you many hours of enjoyment, learning about the history of silver and discovering the intrinsic beauty of one of the world's most precious metals.

Herald Goddard

Joseph Goddard, who founded J. Goddard and Sons Limited in 1839.

Acknowledgements

The author and publishers gratefully acknowledge the help of all those who have lent photographs and given permission for their reproduction in this book. Photographs were supplied courtesy of:
J. H. Bourdon-Smith pages 75, 81 t, 87, 89; Brand Inglis (photo: A. C. Cooper) page 31; The Button Queen (© Elsevier Publishing Projects (UK), photo: P. Forrester) page 149; Chelsea Antiques Fair page 153; Christie's (photos: A. C. Cooper) pages 27, 94, 101 l, 101 r, 102 l, 111, 113; Cooper-Bridgeman Library (photos: A. C. Cooper) pages 23, 24 b, 32 b, 80 l; The Colman Collection of Silver Mustard Pots (photos: J. Blomfield) pages 105 l, 105 r, 106 l, 106 r; Mary Evans Picture Library pages 21 l, 64 l; Garrard and Co pages 13 t, 16 t, 124; Grosvenor House Antiques Fair (photos: Raymond Fortt Studios) pages 92 l, 115 b; Herbert de Gray (photo) page 30 l; Holburne of Menstrie Museum (University of Bath) page 12 r; M. McAleer (© Elsevier Publishing Projects (UK), photo: P. Forrester page 144; Mansell Collection pages 21 r, 62, 64 r, 136; National Museum of Antiquities of Scotland pages 30 r, 44 t; Warden and Fellows of New College, Oxford pages 11 r, 16 b; Phillips Auctioneers pages 13 b, 14, 74, 81 c, 99 l, 99 r, 103, 127 cr, 132 l, 137 c, 137 b, 152 tr, 154 l; S. J. Phillips (© Elsevier Publishing Projects (UK), photo: A. C. Cooper page 18; Picturepoint, London page 90 t; City of Plymouth Museum (photo: Robert Chapman) page 12 l; City of Sheffield Museum (photos: Hallam Design) pages 49, 50, 51, 52, 54 l, 54 r, 55, 56, 57, 59, 60, 151 l; S. J. Shrubsole pages 76 r, 77, 84 t, 151 r – © Elsevier Publishing Projects (UK) photo: P. Forrester; Sir John Soane's Museum (photo: Godfrey New) page 32 t; Somerset House Art Treasures Exhibition page 135 l; Sotheby's Belgravia pages 25, 34 l, 34 r, 35, 36, 65, 67, 68, 76 l, 108, 117, 119 t, 122 t, 122 c, 123 c, 123 br, 126, 127 t, 127 cl, 132 r, 135 r, 137 t, 138 l, 139, 143 tr, 143 b, 148, 152 tl, 152 b; Sotheby's New Bond Street pages 123 t, 123 b; Spink and Son pages 80 r – © Elsevier Publishing Projects (UK), photo: P. Forrester – 89 r, 93; Strata Design pages 39, 40, 41 t, 42, 43, 44 b, 45; Victoria and Albert Museum, Crown Copyright pages 11 l, 15, 17, 24 t, 29 l, 29 r, 37, 38, 41 b, 67 l, 73, 81 b, 83 l, 83 r, 85, 86, 90 bl, 90 br, 91 t, 91 b, 97, 102 r, 104 t, 104 b, 107, 109 l, 109 r, 112, 114 l, 114 r, 115 t, 116 l, 118, 119 b, 120, 122 bl, 122 br, 123 bl, 125 l, 125 r, 128, 129 t, 129 bl, 129 br, 130 l, 130 r, 131, 133, 134 t, 138 r, 140, 141 l, 142, 143 tl, 145 l, 145 r, 146, 147, 150, 154 r, 155 l, 155 r, 156; Yorkshire Museum page 9. (Key: t=top; c=centre; b=bottom; l=left; r=right).

Colour page 1: top: Picturepoint, London; centre left: M. McAleer, © Elsevier Publishing Projects (UK), photo P. Forrester; centre right: S. J. Shrubsole, © Elsevier Publishing Projects (UK), photo P. Forrester; bottom: Spink and Son, © Elsevier Publishing Projects (UK), photo P. Forrester. Colour page 2: top: M. McAleer, © Elsevier Publishing Projects (UK), photo P. Forrester; bottom left: Cooper-Bridgeman Library; bottom right: Victoria and Albert Museum, Crown Copyright. Colour page 3: Victoria and Albert Museum, Crown Copyright. Colour page 4: top: Cooper-Bridgeman Library; bottom left: Victoria and Albert Museum, Crown Copyright; bottom right: Cooper-Bridgeman Library. Colour page 5: top and bottom: M. McAleer, © Elsevier Publishing Projects (UK), photo P. Forrester. Colour page 6: top left: S. J. Phillips, © Elsevier Publishing Projects (UK), photo A. C. Cooper; centre left: Victoria and Albert Museum, Crown Copyright; bottom left: private collection, © Elsevier Publishing Projects (UK), photo P. Forrester; bottom right: Victoria and Albert Museum, Crown Copyright. Colour page 7: top: Cooper-Bridgeman Library; centre left: M. McAleer, © Elsevier Publishing Projects (UK), photo P. Forrester; bottom right: Cooper-Bridgeman Library. Colour page 8: top left: Cooper-Bridgeman Library; bottom left: Phillips Auctioneers; top right: Spink and Son; bottom right: Spink and Son.

Museums with Collections of Silver and Silver Plate

Bath	Holburne of Menstrie Museum (University of Bath), Great Pulteney Street, Bath, Avon, BA2 4DB.
Birmingham	City Museum and Art Gallery, Chamberlain Square, Birmingham, B3 3DH.
Brighton	Preston Manor, Preston Park, Brighton, Sussex, BN1 6SD.
Bristol	City Museum and Art Gallery, Queen's Road, Bristol, Avon, BS8 1RL.
Cardiff	National Museum of Wales, Cathays Park, Cardiff, South Glamorgan, CF1 3NP.
Edinburgh	National Museum of Antiquities of Scotland, Queen Street, Edinburgh, Lothian, EH2 1JD.
Edinburgh	Royal Scottish Museum, Chambers Street, Edinburgh, Lothian, EH1 1JF.
Glasgow	The McLellan Galleries, Glasgow, Strathclyde.
Leeds	Lotherton Hall, Leeds, West Yorkshire.
Leicester	Museum and Art Gallery, New Walk, Leicester.
London	British Museum, Great Russell Street, London, WC1B 3DG.
London	Victoria and Albert Museum, Exhibition Road, London, SW7 2RL.
Norwich	Castle Museum, Norwich, Norfolk, NR1 3JU.
Nottingham	City Art Gallery and Museum, Nottingham Castle, Nottingham.
Oxford	Ashmolean Museum, Beaumont Street, Oxford, OX1 2PH.
Plymouth	City Museum and Art Gallery, Drake Circus, Plymouth, Devon, PL4 8AJ.
Sheffield	City Museum, Weston Park, Sheffield, S10 2TP.

Introduction

Practically every conceivable type of domestic and social object has been made in silver since the Restoration of Charles II in 1660, and this provides a vast field from which collectors may choose. It not only embraces rare, esoteric objects and silver of a luxurious nature, but also a wide range of later items for the collector with less to spend and many pieces which may still be used in the home today. Silver has one enormous advantage over ceramics or glass: should it become irreparable due to an accident, it will always have a melted-down value.

True antiques were made prior to 1830, which was about the time when mass-production methods finally began to oust hand-craftsmanship. For many years anything made after this date was ignored by purists and, because of this, sterling silver pieces produced prior to 1830 were, and still are, increasingly expensive. Their high cost, combined with the growing scarcity of certain types of items, has led to Victorian and specific kinds of twentieth century items at last being taken seriously in the field of antiques. Many of these are now regarded as highly collectable and have become consequently more expensive and scarce. It is, therefore, from the objects which will in turn replace these that the collector with modest means could start a collection. Prices of many such objects are still comparatively low and if chosen with care may prove to be a sound investment.

Certain types of nineteenth century, and sometimes later, electro-plated objects are creeping into the field embraced by the term collectable, and electro-plate prices can be very realistic. Because of this there is a chapter in this book devoted to electro-plate intended for those who wish to start in a small way.

Electro-plate must not be confused with Sheffield plate, however, which has been avidly collected for many years with a corresponding rise in prices. Nevertheless, it is considerably cheaper than sterling silver. Early Sheffield plate incorporated a good surface layer of silver, although this may have partially worn away over the years to reveal the soft glow of copper beneath, which is considered an added attraction by many collectors. This book also contains a special chapter on Sheffield plate for those who are interested in this distinctive type of plate which originated during the fourth decade of the eighteenth century. It is reasonable to expect that good earlier examples will be higher in price and more difficult to find, later examples less so.

A word here about optimism, a subject which is not generally discussed in a book of this kind. I wish to mention it because I consider optimism a vital quality for the true collector. Those who do not possess it should try to cultivate it, since without optimism and a certain buoyancy of spirit, collecting can be deprived of much of its joy, not to mention fraught with periodic anxieties. The optimist will dismiss with a light wave of the hand the negative remark that 'there are no more bargains left'.

Remember, too, that more good buys – and more pleasure generally – will come your way if you are alert. A few passing words caught at a social function about a certain market or shop which specialises in particular objects, or which sells at reasonable prices is always worth investigation. Any unfamiliar objects picked up when browsing should be researched as soon as possible. In this way not only is your knowledge extended but the possibility of missing a bargain is eliminated. Slowly your experience and acquisitions will grow.

Of the small objects which collectors may still find reasonably priced, the following deserve mention although it must be pointed out that, while these may be termed as 'reasonable' at the time of writing, the position can quickly change. Prices can sometimes rise very rapidly in the world of antiques, but seldom does the reverse occur. Small collectable objects, therefore, include later thimbles, Victorian and Edwardian novelty pens and pen holders, propelling pencils and silver sheaths into which black-lead pencils slide, miscellaneous silver-mounted objects, small glass jars with silver lids, button hooks, bookmarkers, certain penknives, fruit knives, tiny stamp boxes, napkin rings, certain sugar tongs, spoons and vesta boxes.

This list excludes items made during the eighteenth and first few decades of the nineteenth century, but even some of these may not be ultimately beyond the reach of those beginning their collection. For, having built up a collection of less expensive items, adding to it when funds permit, many collectors then either sell at a profit, using the money to buy something of more importance, or trade in part exchange with a dealer for something more expensive. It is this incentive to improve a collection which can turn collecting into a life-long habit. There is always something better to which one can aspire and always something of interest to be learned along the way.

Elizabeth de Castres

Part 1 AN INTRODUCTION TO SILVER

1 | A Brief History of Silver

Silver has trodden a continuous and lustrous path through the history of civilisation, its durability and beauty long outliving the ancient men who first formed it into crude wares and ornaments. When Christianity eventually won recognition, silver was a natural choice for the decoration of the Christian Church. The conversion of the British to Christianity spread under the inspired influence of St Augustine and, following the arrival of various missionaries from Ireland, resulted in the need for places of worship in England, appropriately decorated and furnished with sacred vessels. The Irish missionaries brought with them to the north of England tangible proof of their own impressive forms of Christian art, much of which was derived from that on the Continent. Intermingled ornament embracing animal forms which originate directly from such Irish art can be observed on stone crosses which were produced in the north of England. Decoration based on such forms continued during following centuries.

The Ormside Bowl, late eighth century, silver-gilt, decorated with birds and animals amongst a vine scroll. The bowl, with studs of dark blue glass set in its interior, was found buried in the churchyard at Ormside, Cumbria, and may have been placed there by the clergy in the ninth century to conceal it from plundering Vikings.

Sadly, the silver and copper-gilt Ormside Bowl made in the late eighth century, which is in the possession of the Yorkshire Museum, remains alone to show us the sort of workmanship of the period in that part of the country. Rare examples exist from other parts of the country, with much-debated origins. For although there are contemporary records of the quantities of plate, both secular and ecclesiastical, then being produced, none of it remains today. Worcester Cathedral received an impressive silver dish from the King of Mercia at the beginning of the ninth century, and it is also known that King Egbert and King Ethelwulf took plate with them as gifts to Rome. There is little doubt that Anglo-Saxon goldsmiths – the word goldsmith is used in its generic sense throughout this book – were already establishing for themselves a reputation as fine craftsmen even in those remote times, if one can judge by the many papal orders for English plate which they were fulfilling.

Among these goldsmiths was a monk called Dunstan, born in 924, whose fine work included censers, vessels and crosses for his own abbey as well as other pieces. He was to become Archbishop of Canterbury and was later canonised and made the patron, protector and founder of the goldsmiths of London and all England. His effigy, of silver-gilt set with gems, was kept in the hall of the London goldsmiths, their corporate plate also being engraved with his image. When a date letter was added to the London hallmarks in 1478, this was changed annually on 19 May, St Dunstan's Day (see chapter 4).

By the ninth and tenth centuries Scandinavian influences predominated in the north-east of Britain, design being characterised by asymmetrical ribbon patterns mingled with animal outlines. Within the next 100 years this was largely superseded by a German influence, a style which was embellished with paste jewels or precious stones. Byzantine influence also continued.

After the Norman Conquest in 1066, Britain gradually began to settle down under the influence of the French, and the culture of France not unnaturally emerged as the dominant one. Little silver and gold survives from the Dark Ages, particularly that owned by abbeys and churches, since much of this fell into the hands of the Norman conquerors, either as payments to meet various demands or to secure goodwill. It is known that later a large quantity was given by churches towards the ransom of Richard I, and in 1338 Edward III borrowed an enormous amount from certain abbeys and cathedrals. Melted-down silver and gold was in constant demand.

While much of the rare, early work has proved difficult to date and place accurately, the type of decoration and comparison with the ornament found on other contemporary pieces has often been a strong indication of the country and approximate date. Intermingled foliage was still popular in conjunction with animal and human figures on elaborate work of the twelfth century. Ornamental lettering, often in the form of inscriptions in Gothic or Lombardic lettering, perhaps in Latin or French, was commonly engraved on mazers, chalices or cups from mediæval times. The words might be separated by ornamental motifs. Decorative effects used during the fifteenth century were generally related to those on ecclesiastical architecture of the time. Human figures were a particular

source of inspiration as can be seen from the giant salt of All Souls' College, Oxford, with figures of huntsmen and hounds gathered around the feet of a predominant bearded figure. The pedestal of the famous monkey salt owned by New College, Oxford, is supported by four wild men on cushions. The monkey or chimpanzee sits upon another cushion, carrying the rock crystal bowl upon its head.

Such standing salts are among the most important and impressive pieces of all mediæval silver, and a few examples of this extremely fine craftsmanship remain, exquisitely worked and decorated. They represent a social ritual long outmoded which was of great significance during the Middle Ages and for some time to follow. During the fifteenth and sixteenth centuries dining-table etiquette related particularly to rank, and title was allotted much thought. A distinct list of rules was commonly obeyed to maintain the right priorities afforded to each social strata, and relevant books of the period deal with these conclusively. A servant was instructed to set the principal salt on the right of the head of the house at the high table, the second and less important salt at the lower end of the table, and smaller salts on other tables.

Mediæval standing salts were elaborate and imaginative, taking many fantastic forms, often in the shape of animals. Those listed in inventories included dogs, elephants, lions, monkeys and dragons. Sixteenth century salts evolved into more formal pieces, usually with fine proportions and influenced by Renaissance architectural design. A drum shape embossed

Above left: the silver-gilt Campion Cup, made in London and dated 1500, engraved with the words 'Soli deo honor et gloria' in Lombardic lettering.

Above right: the Monkey Salt, New College, Oxford.

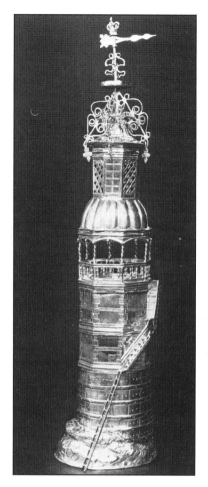 

Far left: the Eddystone Salt, 1698, modelled after the original lighthouse.

Left: silver-gilt Bell Salt, 1613.

with strapwork and contemporary design was also popular, with a domed cover topped by an ornate finial. Many such salts were made during the Elizabethan period, and it is interesting to note that similar pieces, expensive as they were, had already begun to appear in the homes of the wealthy, such as clergy of higher rank and gentry, as distinct from the nobles of the land. Another shape which appeared at the end of the sixteenth century was the bell salt, shaped as its name implies like a bell, generally about ten inches in height, and consisting of three sections, the bottom two being salt cellars while the uppermost part consisted of a small pierced ball-type pepper caster. The salt in its entirety was supported on three ball feet and sometimes ball-and-claw feet.

Other types of mediæval plate included fine standing cups; mazers, a more common type of mediæval drinking vessel, bowl-like without a stem, made of wood, usually maple, measuring from five to about twelve inches in diameter, sometimes with cast feet and decorated on the silver or silver-gilt mounts; drinking horns, the horn beautifully polished and mounted with silver; beakers, an ancient form of drinking vessel; ewers and basins, the latter essential for use at the table when hands needed to be washed because forks were not used at that time, and the former holding scented water for the purpose, carried by pages with napkins for drying the hands; and spoons, both for ecclesiastical use and a few for domestic purposes, intended for spooning food into the mouth and regarded as a most valuable personal possession which would be bequeathed to close relatives. Most of the rare examples of the above-mentioned items are in the possession of colleges, churches, museums and distinguished bodies.

The use of silver grew enormously after Henry VIII came to the throne and in the reign of successive monarchs. And although it was the royal family and nobles who amassed the largest and most magnificent collections of plate, certain types of smaller pieces now began to filter through to wealthy but less important homes. One reason for this was that production in the silver mines of Germany and Central Europe greatly increased by the beginning of the sixteenth century, and later both gold and silver began to be imported from Spanish America in larger quantities. This increase in readily-available bullion meant that the price fell proportionately. Henry VIII was a lavish spender and the court followed his example: fortunes were invested in vast hoards of gold, silver-gilt, silver and jewels. Sometimes this would be for the sovereign's personal use, while on other occasions it would be for a different sort of 'investment', taking the form of gifts for foreign monarchs, their ministers or advisers. Elizabeth I thought fit to give many such costly presents, and was quite happy to order plate to the value of over £10,000 for such reasons when she thought it necessary.

Thus, in addition to the silver objects already mentioned which were being produced during the mediæval period, there now appeared various other vessels. Important among these were two-handled cups and covers, closely related to the loving cups which appeared in the seventeenth and eighteenth centuries, which were passed from one person to another as each in turn took a swig. There were as well smaller versions. The wine cup without a cover, which was purely an individual piece intended for one person only, was smaller and unimportant compared with the splendour of its two-handled bigger brother.

The tankard was a sixteenth century name for a new drum-shaped drinking vessel with a hinged cover, thumbpiece and scrolled handle, and this term gradually replaced the older word 'can'. The vessel, probably of German or Scandinavian origin, might be made of horn and mounted in silver-gilt. One rare tankard with a glass body is in the possession of Clare College, Cambridge, and its silver mounts are hallmarked for 1570. From about this time also metal tankards came into more general use. Superb Elizabethan examples might be decorated with flower and foliate patterns and were quite often gilded.

Top: Elizabeth I flagon, one of a pair, dated 1601.

Above, left to right: a Roman spoon *circa* fifth century; a diamond knop spoon, seventeenth century; an acorn knop spoon, fifteenth century.

Standing dishes upon a stem to hold fruit or other appropriate foods began to appear at about this time, and there was a further increase in spoons, still used for spooning food into the mouth, their knops being variously shaped at the terminal of the stem. A few knives – apart from those used for carving – might be found in the homes of the highest in the land, nobility or clergy, and were among the few highly-esteemed personal possessions to be carried for eating requirements.

There was a gradual increase in the number of silver candlesticks, one of the earliest of which was made during the last four decades of the sixteenth century. The advertisement for the state lottery held in 1567 illustrated among its prizes silver candlesticks with sockets, short stems, wide grease pans and spreading bases, and this is believed to be the first mention of socket candlesticks made of silver. Wall sconces might be used and glittered abundantly on the walls of the palaces and great houses, as did those at a reception given by Cardinal Wolsey in 1527 for the French Ambassador at Hampton Court, which is not surprising since Wolsey's collection of silver and gold was rumoured to have been as extensive as that of Henry VIII. Pepper casters are occasionally recorded at this time as a separate piece, although they were usually incorporated in the salt as already described. But such containers became more necessary as the taste for highly-spiced food became more prevalent during the Elizabethan era and pepper was sold increasingly.

The first sugar refinery was built in England in the sixteenth century. By 1750 more than 30,000 tons were being produced annually, although sugar had been known in England for very much longer. The forerunners of the present-day sugar bowl were beautiful Stuart sugar boxes and covered bowls which, although rare, may still be seen today at better silver dealers or museums.

Of the enormous amount of magnificent silver and gold produced for the Church during the early years of the sixteenth century, little remains due to the suppression of the monasteries and the Reformation. Sadly, also, very few pieces of domestic silver survive. They were probably

Shell-shaped sugar or spice box, *circa* 1609.

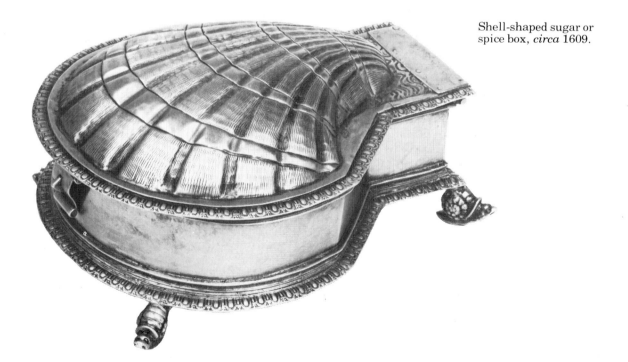

melted down with changes in fashion and fortune, and today we are left usually only with written evidence of such pieces in the form of statements in inventories, letters or similar records.

From the accession to the throne in 1603 of James I and throughout the proceeding years up to the Protectorate, a continuation in the trends already mentioned was maintained. One or two additional pieces included an obscure vessel in the form of a tankard or cup, to one side of which was soldered a tube which ended in a spout. Its true purpose has not been ascertained, but since these spout cups were also found in ceramics, they must have served a definite purpose for the pouring of some sort of liquid. Another new vessel was a rudimentary type of punch bowl which took the form of a larger type of two-handled cup and cover, and is worth noting because of the way it illustrates the sometimes halting progress of evolution in wares, since the monteith, which did not make its appearance until several years later, is usually regarded as the forerunner of the punch bowl.

Flagons, wine cups and goblets were much in demand, and the wine taster began to appear more commonly among the smaller vessels. These shallow bowl-like objects had been employed since the fourteenth and fifteenth centuries, when English vintners had used them when visiting the wine cellars of the Continent. In a statute of 1477 which prohibited the export of silver, exception was made to this small, useful vessel. Sixteenth century records show an increase in their use, and it is thought by some that they may have had other purposes, perhaps more generally as a vessel for brandy or spirits, even though wine tasting had already

Spout cup made in Norwich, *circa* 1642.

become quite a specialised profession. Numerous examples of wine cups and goblets remain today. Generally made before the Civil War, they were usually about five to ten inches in height, standing upon baluster stems and with variously shaped bowls. An interesting change now began to take place in the shape of spoons, their bowls becoming generally more oval, and their stem terminals sometimes made without decoration (knop) which until this time was usual. A short 'V' tongue began to appear at the back of the bowl to strengthen it.

With the Restoration in 1660 and a growing prosperity came the unleashing of a frenzied desire for luxury. There was an incredible demand for English domestic silver, and, in addition, a need to replace ecclesiastical and certain ceremonial pieces lost or melted down during the Civil War. Ninety per cent of this silver was made in London. The royal palaces glistered and gleamed with vast quantities of opulent and splendid silver, emulated by the nobles and wealthier citizens right through to the taverners whose usage of silver tankards, basins, cups and bowls resulted in so many robberies that an Act was passed which forbade them to expose in public all wrought or manufactured plate, except spoons. The demand for silver embraced many diverse types of

Above: a rare silver spice jar, one of a pair, maker's mark IB, made in 1675.

Left: beaker, made in London, *circa* 1680.

utensils and objects, therefore, from grand ceremonial pieces to the modest beaker. It also included incredible pieces of heavy, silver furniture of immense weight and value.

Standing cups, many of which are still in the possession of their original owners, became a usual form of presentation gift to colleges, City companies or similar concerns. Two-handled cups and covers were made in increasing numbers, many of which survive today, but silver wine cups decreased as a result probably of the growing use of English crystalline glass for this purpose. Beakers and mugs in different forms continued to be made, many for Oxford and Cambridge colleges, and such college cups are known by varying names including 'tuns'. Tankards developed in numerous ways during this period, and their use became more general. An interesting addition to the range of drinking vessels during the second half of the seventeenth century was the tumbler cup. The monteith also came into being in about 1684, an early example of which is in the possession of King's College, Cambridge.

The largest vessel associated with the serving of wine also made its appearance. This was the enormous wine cistern, almost the size of a small bath, which was used to contain the bottles of wine at banquets or other grand functions. One such example, made for the Duke of Rutland in 1681, measured four feet in length and 18 inches in height and weighed some 3,000 ounces. Another was bequeathed by Sarah, first Duchess of Marlborough, to her granddaughter Lady Diana Spencer, but was far smaller since it was intended for use on a sideboard or side-table. Although wine cisterns were intended primarily for bottles, their general use may have included washing up at social functions, since certain comments in contemporary literature suggest this. The wine fountain, unlike the cistern, was filled with wine and usually placed on a side-table. Its splendour was none the less impressive and much beloved by the élite who made a point of spending lavishly on such prestigious items.

An important new beverage which made its appearance at about this time was responsible for the introduction of a vital piece of domestic silver to which we have long grown accustomed. An advertisement for this appeared in the *London Gazette* in 1658 and is most likely the earliest reference to tea. Two years later Samuel Pepys was recording in his diary his first 'cup of tee'. At the same time tea was being sold in leaf at around 15 shillings (75p) to 50 shillings (£2·50) a pound. An Act of Parliament levied a duty of eightpence (about 3½p) on every gallon of tea made for sale. Nevertheless by 1678 imports were amounting to 4,713 pounds, and within approximately two decades of the following century this had grown to more than 1,000,000 pounds. But there was no sign of anything resembling a teapot in silver until several years after the diary entry made by Samuel Pepys. The earliest-known example was made some ten years later and can be seen at the Victoria and Albert Museum, London. It bears little comparison to the teapot as we know it, examples of which were not made until the beginning of the eighteenth century.

The earliest-known type of silver teapot, dated 1670.

Coffee was first introduced into England as early as 1637. By 1650 the first coffee house had opened in Oxford and within about 30 years the number had grown to several hundred in London. As with tea, a vessel was needed for the new beverage, and the coffee pot was introduced. A rare and early specimen, made in 1681, is also in the Victoria and Albert Museum. Chocolate, another new and fashionable beverage, was poured from a pot similar to that used for coffee.

By the end of the seventeenth century the standing salt, used for so many generations and of great social importance, was declining in popularity because of the recent preference for eating in dining rooms instead of large, communal halls. In place of the standing salt came the salt cellar, early examples of which were utilitarian, trencher salts, the basic forerunners of the decorative cellars which were to appear in the eighteenth century. At about the same time the silver fork made a gradual appearance, its stem resembling that of contemporary spoons, and with three prongs instead of four, the latter number not generally appearing until after about 1674. With the growing number of silver candlesticks came an increase in the number of candle snuffers made in silver. Tapersticks were also produced in silver towards the end of this period as were inkstands (standishes), sugar bowls, sumptuous toilet sets and expensive miniature toys.

The eighteenth century saw the gradual evolution or arrival of practically all the domestic silver we now take for granted, in addition to many objects which no longer have a job to fulfil in the home, since progress has rendered them unnecessary. Such pieces still possess much charm and are no less collected than more ubiquitous objects such as the

Mustard pot by Eliza Godfrey, *circa* 1755.

mustard pot. Mustard is an ancient plant, long relished with a variety of meats. During the fifteenth century a piquant mustard sauce was much favoured with brawn, beef, bacon and mutton, while a mustard-and-sugar concoction often accompanied pheasant. Mustard-makers were mentioned in records during the fifteenth and sixteenth centuries, and while one of the earliest references to a mustard pot occurs in 1380, mustard pots as we know them did not appear until approximately 1724, becoming more generally used after the middle of the eighteenth century. Mass-production methods brought them, in common with other pieces of domestic silver, within the reach of a wider public by the last years of the eighteenth century.

The tea caddy, the earliest examples of which appeared in the final years of the seventeenth century, likewise grew more common as the eighteenth century progressed, as did tea kettles, sugar bowls (sugar plantation owners accumulated such vast wealth that in the mid-eighteenth century sugar was known as 'white gold'), milk jugs, caddy spoons (produced in an amazing quantity and variety during the final years of the eighteenth century and into the nineteenth century), dessert and table spoons, knives and forks, fish servers, ladles, sugar tongs, cake and fruit baskets, trays, sauceboats, toast racks and numerous other items. Certain more specialised objects came into being, such as the vinaigrette, a small box containing a sponge soaked in an aromatic vinegar which was the forerunner of the bottle of smelling salts, and the nutmeg grater, a portable little box containing a nutmeg and rasp.

The story of silver is thus a full and fascinating one, playing an important role in the history of civilisation. Those who could never have hoped to own such a precious metal could admire it in their places of worship. Today we are luckier for we can also see it in the ancient houses throughout the land and observe it at leisure in our museums.

2 The Working and Decoration of Silver

Pure silver, like pure gold, is far too soft a metal to be used satisfactorily for making coins, wares, ornaments, jewellery and other objects. To make it viable for everyday use, therefore, it is necessary to harden it and this is done by alloying it with a base metal which also makes it more workable. The base metal alloyed with silver is usually copper. In England this alloy consists of 11 ounces 2 dwt (pennyweights) of silver and 18 dwt of copper to each Troy pound (there are 12 ounces to the Troy pound) which is 925 parts fine, and which, with one exception, has been the legal standard for sterling silver since 1300 (see chapter 3).

Thus when a piece is described as being made of sterling silver this means that it is virtually solid silver. Plated silver, with which this book also deals in detail, therefore, can never be anywhere near the quality of sterling silver, even though it may have much to commend it in its own right. The word sterling, chosen to describe the legal standard of silver, has simple origins and has been used since mediæval times when the amount of silver used in wares and other objects had to equal that of sterlings or silver pence, the currency in use at that time (see chapter 4).

When the silver had been alloyed with 18 dwt of copper, early goldsmiths needed to set about the task of making it into a workable sheet of metal. This was done by laboriously hammering the ingot into a metal sheet, the gauge or thickness of which would enable it to be formed into wares. For this purpose brute force and a sledge-hammer were required. Later, rather less arduously, a rolling-mill was used. Then came the more skilful part of the procedure, that of forming the vessels. This was usually done quite simply by cutting appropriately-sized round pieces of metal from the sheet, and then 'raising' them into the hollow shapes of the required vessels by careful hammering on the sinking block which would be shaped to fit the outlines of various vessels, or on stakes made of iron or steel. A particular type of hammer devoid of sharp edges was used since it was vital not to disfigure the silver in any way. Also, since the metal tended to become springy and thus more difficult to work during the technique, it needed to be annealed from time to time as the work progressed.

Eventually, when the craftsman was satisfied with the shape, and after constant measuring with calipers and gauges, the next step would be undertaken. This also required skill and patience, and consisted of polishing or planishing the piece until its finest lustre was attained. This was achieved by careful hammering with a broad-faced polished hammer which also gradually smoothed out any irregularities in the surface of

the metal. When the main body of the vessel was completed, additional parts such as spouts, handles, feet or finials would be cast in moulds and soldered to the body with silver solders which had a lower melting temperature than the silver alloy used in the vessel. Certain vessels such as tankards would also be made in two horizontal sections and soldered together, the join being concealed by some form of decoration. Another technique also used for beakers consisted of making a cylinder shape with a vertical join and inserting a base in the bottom (see chapter 11).

Decoration was achieved in various ways, and the methods used altered little over the years. The most common technique of all was engraving which was an ancient form of ornament often very simply applied. A scorper – a small chisel with blades of various shapes – or graver would be used to cut decorative lines out of the metal, removing the silver in the process. Flat chasing gave a similar appearance, the craftsman hammering punches along the surface of the metal, which achieved a less well-defined effect but did not remove any of the metal. The pattern could generally be discerned faintly on the reverse side of the metal. While working with his hammer and punch the craftsman would manage to keep the hollow vessel in shape by filling it with pitch amalgam. The engraver worked the metal on a firm pad, which was usually covered with some sort of leather since less force was required to cut away the metal than was needed for flat chasing.

Punching and embossing were other methods of decoration. The former would be achieved by applying with one stroke a punch with a plain or shaped head, while the latter required the pressure of the punches to be applied from the reverse side of the metal. More involved patterns which were applied from the reverse of the metal, usually in conjunction with

Above left: silversmiths at work, *circa* 1700.

Above right: raising a circular sheet of silver by hammering it on a stake.

chasing, are generally termed 'repoussé'. Other decorative effects were achieved in a variety of ways, one of which would be by filling the grooves cut by the engraver with a black alloy called niello, giving the overall engraved pattern a clearly-defined contrast. This is usually found on smaller pieces. Opaque and translucent enamels were also similarly employed, described as champlevé or cloisonné. The first term is used when the places to be filled are cut away with a scorper, and the second when voids are contained within wire soldered to the surface to make channels.

Piercing, which is a process whereby pieces of the metal are cut away leaving the remainder in the form of a pattern, was accomplished originally by the use of a fret-saw, a small hole first being made in the metal so that the fret-saw could be inserted. The whole procedure was a comparatively tedious job since the saw needed to be constantly sharpened because the steel from which it was made was not hard enough to cope with the necessary friction. Progress later brought about harder steels. Piercing resulting from this crude method required to be strengthened since so much silver was cut away, and this was usually done by convex embossing. The cut edges also had to be smoothed considerably before the job was finished. By the 1770s advances in mechanism brought about an improved stamping machine and, by altering the punches, this could be used to cut simple open-work patterns. Such piercing was used increasingly for objects such as sugar baskets, or fruit and cake baskets, incorporating neo-classical motifs which were soldered on by hand. Not many years were to pass before these motifs, too, were incorporated in the automatically cut-out pattern. The steel tool which the fly-press incorporated, and which pierced the sheet of silver, was later made of a harder steel, which meant that it could make longer runs and also produce more elaborate patterns.

Applied ornament used in a variety of ways was also popular. It included patterns cut from sheets of silver or decorative castings which were soldered to the main body of the object. The former type is exemplified by cut-card work which became fashionable from around the last decade or so of the seventeenth century until about 1720, and is attributed mainly to emigré Huguenot silversmiths, although it was known in England as early as approximately 1667, since it can be seen on a pair of covered cups of this date at the Ashmolean Museum, Oxford. For this type of applied ornament, pieces of silver were cut from another sheet of silver – often in the form of a leaf – and soldered to the vessel with considerable skill, because the craftsman thus had to ensure that the solder was at precisely the right temperature. This applied decoration then showed in relief against the surface of the vessel.

Originally cut-card work was comparatively simple and usually narrow, in foliate patterns. It was used generally to decorate a vessel above the foot-ring, on lids or covers and was sometimes applied lavishly over the lower half of the body. It might also be used to strengthen certain weak areas such as junctions, where a handle might be joined by solder to the main body. Later, as the skill of the goldsmith increased, cut-card work became more complicated and separate leaves might be soldered one upon the other to give a particularly delicate standing-proud effect. A

Cut-card work, *circa* 1715.

further progression was to engrave or chase the applied metal. Leaves might thus be engraved with veins or mid-ribs. Other types of embellishment for cut-card work included the application of cast additions, perhaps cast mid-ribs applied as a third layer, or small beading. Piercing might also be used but generally only appears on more superior work.

Gilding was a technique used to cover silver with gold, and various methods were employed in this process. One was to melt the gold and mix it with mercury, extracting the excess of mercury and painting the mixture onto the surface of the silver with a brush, then removing the rest of the mercury by evaporating it with heat, leaving the gold fused to the silver. The disadvantage to this was that mercury vapour is poisonous. Another method eliminated this vapour. A cloth previously soaked in a solution of chloride of gold was completely dried and burnt, the resultant ashes being rubbed onto the surface of the silver to which they stuck. Gilding was also applied at a later stage by electrolysis.

An important step forward in mechanisation and one which was ultimately to influence greatly the making of silver wares appeared in the very final years of the seventeenth century. This was the English invention of the new metal rolling-mill, which for a while had little effect on the manufacture of silver. It was greatly improved upon, however, during the third decade of the eighteenth century when compressing springs were added to the upper of the two revolving cylinders. Thus it was possible to put an unheated ingot of silver through rollers which would eventually flatten the metal into a sheet of uniform gauge. For the first time objects could be produced in thinner silver which reduced their cost as both the weight of the silver and the time needed to render it down from the ingot were diminished. The rolling-mill was used increasingly as its efficiency improved and it became possible to produce silver of a very thin gauge, which cut costs still further.

By the late 1760s more inventions meant that machinery could be used very successfully for stamping, piercing and embossing, thus rapidly producing wares which had previously taken the craftsman many hours of labour to hammer up from the flat and decorate by hand. The thin silver produced by the rolling-mill was exactly right for automatic stamping by drop-hammers and fly-punches, and parts of vessels were quickly stamped out and soldered together. During the following decade a machine which produced beaded wire was patented. Mass-production grew as greater progress in mechanisation reduced the gauge of the silver, and harder steel increased the speed at which domestic silver could be produced. In fact, silver used in the production of candlesticks in particular was so thin and flimsy that these generally required to be weighted with an interior filling of resins, pitch or ashes.

The new machines were generally driven by water-power, but Matthew Boulton and his partner John Fothergill pioneered the steam-powered rolling-mill and used this with much success in their factory from the 1770s. Boulton and Fothergill, among others, produced unfinished, shaped silver parts in quantity which were bought by silversmiths for assembling and finishing. Thus, in the case of pierced table baskets, for example, a single basket might consist of 20 or 30 different pierced panels, all of which had been automatically pierced by a manufacturing silversmith, and finally made into the finished object by the silversmith.

A candlestick of thin silver with weighted base, Sheffield, 1778.

Costs were as low as they had ever been, bringing domestic silver within the reach of the general public, albeit at the expense of heavier silver and over-all hand-work, both of which were still available to those who wished to pay for such refinements. Master silversmiths in London still raised silver from the ingot by hand and hand-decorated it in the old ways but, because of the unprecedented flow of domestic silver now issuing from Sheffield and Birmingham, the monopoly which London silversmiths had enjoyed for generations at last came to an end. Few people required the individual services which could be provided by master craftsmen and, since by the end of the eighteenth century the possession of domestic silver and cutlery had become an established part of upper-middle class life, the general services of the retailer were now more in demand than the costly personal service provided by the craftsman-silversmith.

Towards the end of the eighteenth century a new type of ornamentation appeared which was to remain in fashion until about 1815. Known as bright-cutting, it consisted of a series of cuts made in the silver by sharp tools of varying sizes, slanted in such a way as to produce a delightful faceted effect. This form of engraving, which was extremely delicate and pretty, was very fashionable during the 1790s, being particularly suited to the neo-classical type of decoration so beloved at this time on practically all pieces of silver, large or small.

Bright-cut decoration on a sugar basket made in 1792.

By the mid-1850s another popular form of decoration was achieved by engine-turning, which is typical of Victorian ornament on certain items such as snuff boxes, card cases or specific types of vinaigrettes. After being turned on the lathe, the object not only acquired a textured effect, but the ridges achieved by the turning also served in their own way as a protection from occasional careless fingering or minor scratches. One of the earliest forms of an ornamental turning lathe used for decoration is the treadle type in the Science Museum, London, which was probably made towards the end of the seventeenth century, although it was not until well into the nineteenth century that the method became

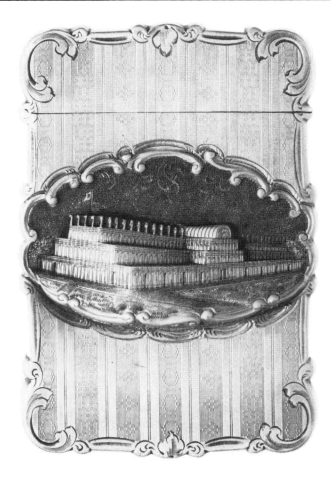

Card case by Nathaniel
Mills, Birmingham,
1850, chased in high
relief and engine-turned,
depicting the Crystal
Palace.

established. Various patterns and designs suitable for small boxes could
be produced on the lathe, including radial engine-turning and other types
of rotary, straight or oval work. During the mid-1840s from Birmingham
came an incredible assortment of vinaigrettes, snuff boxes, card cases
and other boxes which might be first engine-turned by 'engine-cutters',
and then handed over to the craftsman for engraving or other forms of
decoration. Others sometimes featured only engine-turned decoration
and needed no further embellishment, for the quality was generally high.

Acid-etching was a further type of ornament sometimes employed from
about 1830, but known of before this time. Patents were taken out during
the first 40 years or so of the nineteenth century, although artists were
well-acquainted with the technique of etching long before this time. One
such patent was concerned with a new way of preparing particular
surfaces for corrosion with acids which made it easier to produce patterns
and designs for, among other things, printing. The corrosive element was
used to produce some delightful patterns and scenes on silver objects,
giving them interesting 'depth'.

The hinges of boxes were always of great importance, right back to the
first of their kind. Until the early years of the eighteenth century these

were usually of the knuckle-and-lug type, the base incorporating the former component and the lid the latter. The base and the lid would then be joined by a traverse bolt. These early hinges usually stood 'proud' ie stood away from the main body of the object. The eighteenth century hinge moved from its original position at the rim of the box and appeared towards the centre, with suitably symmetrical ornament disguising it. By the end of the century integral hinges had made their appearance. These have long delighted collectors of boxes since they were often hardly seen, so perfectly did they merge into the decoration on the surface of the top of the lid. When the top was lifted it revealed the integral hinge artistically integrated in the general pattern. These hinges were made concurrently with the normal type of hinge and became very popular.

Although the production of vessels by the method of spinning had been known of since ancient times and was used by the Egyptians to make hollow-wares, improvements in the technique during the nineteenth century brought it into more general use. The craftsman or spinner placed a flat silver sheet in the lathe for rotating. The silver was then worked over a shaped chuck made of *lignum vitae* or beech using a long-handled tool with a head made of steel which burnished the silver as it was worked. The silver needed to be annealed during the process as it gradually formed the shape of the chuck.

The techniques of making cutlery (flatware) did not change greatly until the final decades of the eighteenth century. Apart from the early form of spoon (see chapter 1), cutlery was slow to be adopted for use at the table in England. For many years the spoon accompanied the knife, the blade of which was of fine steel usually bearing the bladesmith's mark. These were made mostly in Sheffield and London. Although forks were in use on the Continent the English did not seem to see any particular merit in these at the table, although they had been known as early as Elizabethan days. They did not start to become generally used until the following century, when they took their natural place as the complement of the knife. At this time their stems were hammered flat. Although matching knives and forks with silver hafts were produced for many years from the beginning of the reign of George I, the solid silver was cumbersome to use since it was so heavy. With the improvements in the rolling-mill and the resultant thin silver, the manufacture of cutlery began to take on a new character. From the 1770s the hafts of knives and forks were stamped out from this cheaper, thinner silver in their thousands, and business in Sheffield thus accelerated. The hafts were die-struck in two parts and then soldered together. Shellac was poured into the completed haft thus formed, and the tang of the blade or fork would then be fixed securely inside the haft before the shellac hardened.

A survey of the men employed in the business of working precious metals, excluding those who produced watch cases, buckles, buttons and other small items, was made in 1773, and of the 307 names mentioned, 24 were described as haft- and hilt-makers, 27 as spoon-makers, 156 as goldsmiths and 96 as plateworkers. This last figure was indicative of future trends. The large percentage of plateworkers continued during the following century with the introduction of electro-plate.

While both Sheffield plate and electro-plate are dealt with at length in

their relevant chapters, one important difference which existed between these two types of plating should be noted in this chapter. In the manufacture of Sheffield plate, it was first made in the sheet and *then* into wares, while in the manufacture of electro-plate, the wares were made first, then placed in the vat for electro-plating. Thus items made chiefly of Sheffield plate might sometimes have component parts made in sterling silver as in the case of candelabra which might have stems or branches of Sheffield plate and mounts of silver.

Although methods of mass-production increased from the last three decades of the eighteenth century reaching a zenith with the Industrial Revolution of the nineteenth century, there was a return by certain craftsmen within 100 years or so to the hand-made techniques employed by early silversmiths (see chapter 3). These craftsmen emulated the methods of their predecessors and because of this the wares which they produced were outstanding among the welter of machine-made Victorian silver with its disregard for simplicity of form. The wares which these designer-silversmiths produced have now become highly-prized collector's pieces, as indeed probably will the hand-made silver objects of merit being made today.

Flatware, *circa* 1713 and 1714, the steel blades of the later knives stamped with the bladesmith's mark.

Changes in Style Through the Years

3

Everybody has a favourite style and type of decoration, and knowing a particular period well can be of great help to the collector. After a while he may be able to tell at a glance approximately when a piece was made, and perhaps, if his expertise has grown sufficiently, who made the object. To be able to do this is not only immensely useful and satisfying, it also has the added advantage that the collector no longer has to rely purely on hallmarks. The English system of hallmarking is one of which we can be justly proud. It has well stood the test of time since its introduction in the Middle Ages. Nevertheless, frauds do exist: for example, hallmarks can be taken from their original pieces and placed on other objects in such a way as to mislead even the experienced collector. Because of this a thorough knowledge of style and decoration may prevent ultimate disappointment in a piece.

The Restoration of the Monarchy in 1660 saw a rekindling of interest in beauty and design, and an excess of domestic silver became the norm among the nobility and wealthy. According to J. F. Hayward in his book *Huguenot Silver in England*, the Earl of Devonshire paid over £1,200 for a massive silver wine cistern which weighed 3,496 ounces. His account from which this entry (1687) is taken shows that at that time he purchased nearly 5,000 ounces of silver. All of this would have been made into objects by the best craftsmen of the day, taking particular care over design, ornament and style. The most popular type of decoration on silver at this time generally consisted of elaborate embossed work, comprising flowers used in conjunction with scrolls or spiralling foliate patterns, animals, birds and fruit. Other popular motifs included classical-inspired formal designs of acanthus leaves and the popular use of fluting, typical of the style referred to as William and Mary, the half-round channels – vertical, oblique or spiral – terminating with a simple motif, perhaps a quatrefoil or trefoil.

Chinoiseries were another form of ornament much beloved towards the end of the seventeenth century and originating, it is believed, from the Chinese porcelain wares or lacquer work then being imported into England. These took the form of quaint but charming Oriental figures against an appropriate background, painstakingly copied by English craftsmen who, nevertheless, seemed to have had their own ideas about Oriental looks and embellishments, since their own quaint interpretations are often incorporated. These chinoiseries have a sort of primitive charm which adds greatly to their attraction. They were usually flat chased, greatly resembling engraving. They started to appear

on silver from about 1670, and have been copied intermittently ever since, although never with the same disarmingly fresh approach. Later versions are sometimes prosaically referred to as being 'in the Chinese style' which on the whole is less misleading and is not usually mistaken for the earlier chinoiseries.

An important historical event took place at this time which was greatly to influence the style of London goldsmiths: the Revocation of the Edict of Nantes in 1685, which resulted in thousands of Huguenot craftsmen fleeing to other countries, including England. Among them were masters of their various crafts, including goldsmiths who employed techniques and ideas at that time often unexplored by London goldsmiths. Their arrival was timely in as much as new techniques and styles were needed as never before to meet the enormous demand for domestic silver. Their skill and enterprise was resented by London goldsmiths, however, and for years there was much ill-feeling between the English craftsmen and the Huguenots, whose talent and skill were soon being acclaimed by wealthy patrons. By around 1700, therefore, a French influence began to make itself felt, becoming rapidly more entrenched and quite accepted during the first two decades or so of the eighteenth century.

It was in general a style which was immensely pleasing, decorative but not overwhelming, yet at the same time often richly ornate. It was generally based on ornament cast in high relief in conjunction with heavy mouldings, sometimes gadrooned or fluted, with much exquisitely-applied cut-card work (see chapter 2), at which the Huguenot goldsmiths excelled. At the same time plain, undecorated wares were also being produced, usually by London craftsmen. There was a great demand for this less elaborate silver since Huguenot designs often involved the

Above left: top view of a tazza with fine repoussé work, made in London, *circa* 1664.

Above right: tankard, *circa* 1670, height five inches.

use of more metal, thus increasing the overall cost. Gradually the two styles became less distinct until by about the third decade of the century they had practically merged. Important among the shapes of vessels then was the pyriform or pear shape, either circular or polygonal, which was particularly popular for teapots and sugar casters. A globular (bullet) shape was also fashionable, including the spherical teapot from Scotland.

One of the most outstanding and beautiful periods in the history of domestic silver now reached a peak, much patronised in France and attributed among others to Juste-Aurèle Meissonnier (1695-1750). In their search for a less formal means of expression, such designers turned from French Régence ideas and the late Italianate baroque to explore what became known as the rococo style. This was an imaginative style of utter fantasy, derived from swirling asymmetrical patterns and C- and S-scrolls, reminiscent of the movement of the sea upon sand, with rock and shell motifs. Hence the word rococo from the French word *rocaille* meaning rock-work. It was a complete change from the former, more rigid type of decoration and was immensely popular. As time progressed this decoration became florid and increasingly ebullient, often covering entirely the surfaces of the pieces which it adorned. Under this influence, cut-card work evolved into a more complicated form of strapwork with foliate forms and flowers intermingling. Chinoiseries reappeared but were far more sophisticated and vigorous than the late seventeenth century examples, with flamboyant repoussé work and engraved rococo cartouches. The *bombé* shape, consisting of a rotund upper half curving into a low waist with more slender lower portion, became fashionable in approximately 1750 and was used for various

Above left: sugar caster by Paul de Lamerie, London, 1725.

Above right: spherical Scottish teapot by George Robertson, Aberdeen, *circa* 1725.

examples of both domestic silver and furniture, particularly commodes.

The rococo period had reached an unchallenged peak of popularity which seemed likely to continue, when it was quite suddenly eclipsed by a style entirely different and opposed in every way. This came like a breath of fresh air upon the sea of heavily-encrusted wares which dominated the

Neo-classical bowl by Andrew Fogelberg and Stephen Gilbert, London, 1789.

domestic scene. The neo-classical era had arrived. It began to appear towards the end of the 1760s and by 1770 had achieved such acclaim that its popularity was assured until the end of the century. English travellers, artists and dilettanti had begun to visit the ancient, classical sites of Herculaneum and Pompeii many years before, and had returned with revised ideas on classical art, bringing with them sculpture and pottery. The whole subject was being given new thought, the ideas of the antiquaries of the Renaissance coming under penetrating and critical observation. The publications on the finds and buildings over the 35 years or so from approximately the 1750s provided a great source of inspiration, their appearance from time to time stimulating a renewed interest in classical art, particularly among designers and artists.

Robert Adam, the architect and designer, was among those who had visited Italy during the 1750s. He had stayed in the country for several years, travelling widely, and upon his return to England he was appointed architect to George III. Robert Adam's name will always be associated with the neo-classical revival, many referring to it simply as the Adam period. In the great houses which he built with such strict adherence to classical proportion and ornament, and in his striking sketches for silver (Sir John Soane's Museum, London) one can see immediately how these new, elegant shapes for important presentation cups or grand pieces for the great houses, set the high artistic standard which was emulated throughout the entire range of domestic silver.

The shape of the vessel was the all-important factor in neo-classical design, unlike rococo-inspired pieces which relied instead upon their flamboyant style of decoration. The new classical outlines were composed of flowing curves, perhaps octagonal on a plain, vase shape, tapering gently to the base, a slender stem joining the vessel to the circular, oval or square foot. Other vessels might be straight-sided, delicately engraved, later perhaps bearing delightful bright-cut decoration. Thus in strict contrast to rococo ideas, all was formality and lightness with classical motifs inspired by Greek or Roman ideas. Ornament included shallow fluting, formalised honeysuckle flowers, acanthus leaves, rams' heads, wreaths of leaves, swags of ribbon tied in lazy bows at the centre, elliptical medallions, swags of drapery, beading, astragals and reeding. Whereas rococo ornament had been asymmetrical, neo-classical decoration was founded on pure symmetry. The new ideas seem first to have been used in architecture which then demanded similarly-inspired interior decoration and furniture, followed by silver and ceramics. During the last quarter of the eighteenth century more items of domestic silver and Sheffield plate were produced than at any previous time and practically all were in the neo-classical style.

By around the turn of the nineteenth century the neo-classical fashion was on the wane, and design during the period which followed, which is generally described as Regency, was far more opulent and heavy. That medley of fantasy, Brighton Pavilion, contained furniture and general decorative effects typical of much of the period. Such ideas were commonly based on art and design inspired by ancient Egypt, Greece and Imperial Rome, Gothic architecture and the Far and Near East. Thus the elegant neo-classical style, patronised so intensely during the last three decades or so of the previous century, was superseded by, among others, elaborate ornament inspired by Imperial Rome perhaps combined with Egyptian motifs originating from royal masks and the Sphinx. However, domestic silver produced during the first 15 to 20 years of the nineteenth century relied on repetitive patterns such as the key or foliate bands,

A Robert Adam drawing inscribed 'Vase for Thomas Dundass Esq for a Prize'.

Close-up of a border decoration featuring compound key pattern.

typical of neo-classical decoration, but this silver was not particularly outstanding, the shapes generally being far less elegant than those of the late eighteenth century.

Rococo decorative effects also reappeared with florid C-scrolls, flowers and chinoiseries. This also was seldom up to the standard of eighteenth century rococo, for it seemed somehow to have lost its way and was mostly devoid of the flair and imagination of the 1740s and 1750s. Even worse, many people eager to comply with current fashion sent perfectly good plainer pieces of silver to the silversmith to be embossed with this new revived rococo decoration. By the third decade or so of the nineteenth century the Romantic movement was already apparent on much domestic silver which might be encumbered with a variety of motifs including classical and others borrowed variously from the previous century, combining freely with contemporary ideas, some new, some derived. When well executed the general effect could have an unexpected exuberant quality.

As the young Queen Victoria ascended the throne, therefore, decoration and design were ready to fly off in any direction. The rococo revival increased in popularity and naturalism began to play an important part on the Victorian scene. The new era also saw those characteristics so typical of this period: the tendency to over-exaggerate outlines, and the insatiable appetite for an excess of ornament. Shapes of domestic silver, like its ornament, were derived from earlier examples during the new years of Victoria's reign, but were followed more precisely than most later developments since little regard was paid to such detail, designers producing amazingly fanciful interpretations which generally lacked the proportion and correct form of the vessels they emulated. Thus the rotund half of the familiar pyriform outline, which had first made its appearance at the beginning of the eighteenth century, was given a more exaggerated and pronounced outline, resulting in a squat effect. The classical urn shape, still being produced, evolved into an outline with high shoulders, tapering down to elongated, slender sides which curved out gracefully at the feet incorporated in the general line of the design. A generous embellishment of ornament, curving rims and extremely decorative scroll handles became general throughout domestic silver. In common with preceding generations, Victorians regarded their silver as an important status symbol, and the more decorative or opulent the silver was, the better they liked it. Simplicity was generally shunned, and thus ornament became an eclectic combination, often with outrageous results.

As the Victorian era wore on, not only were there revivals of the main styles but, running concurrently with them, an assortment of others derived and mixed with previous ideas. Decorative motifs were just as varied, but two of great importance were the vine and the acanthus. Early Victorian designs used these with great enthusiasm: leaves and branches of the vine entwined everywhere, often bearing a preponderance of grapes, in conjunction perhaps with convolvulus and periwinkle plants. Naturalism grew fashionable as rapidly as did the plants beneath the craftsman's tools. Great attention was paid to detail so that the plants and flowers would look as realistic as possible. Plates and dishes might also be shaped like leaves, a salt cellar coyly concealing

its true purpose perhaps in the guise of a periwinkle plant. Rococo scrolls might interweave with thistles.

Naturalism in design raced ahead and reached its zenith by the 1840s and into the next decade. Now exotic tropical plants began to join the mundane bunch of grapes. The vine had become commonplace, as had the demure periwinkle. Statuesque palm trees made their appearance, sometimes supporting dishes, or perhaps adding a realistic touch to a group of Arabs. Such ideas developed into a Moorish style as part of a bizarre form of naturalism. Moorish scenes became increasingly fashionable and graced important pieces of silver. Naturalism generally continued as the most popular theme for years, although it came under severe criticism by certain progressive artists and designers. There were few items of domestic silver which were not adorned by it in some form or other, from claret jugs to teapots, around which the vine twisted tenaciously or the rustic 'oak' added a pastoral touch.

Other styles also popular and much beloved of the time included Elizabethan, Gothic and Renaissance decoration. The first was typified by heavy strapwork, commonly found around oval cartouches and engraved on various types of domestic silver. Gothic ornament was derived from various architectural outlines, such as the pointed church arch and stylised foliate designs. Although it was usually reserved for ecclesiastical silver, it also appeared on a miscellany of domestic objects, including tea kettles, teapots and coffee pots.

Renaissance silver directly related to the art of Italian Renaissance metalwork relied for its ornament usually on cast decoration in conjunction with flat chasing and engraving. Small pieces of domestic silver might be more simply decorated. Renaissance design grew in popularity during the 1850s and was used on opulent centrepieces and candelabra. Other pieces might be decorated with a mixture of classical-inspired as well as Renaissance motifs.

Above left: wine coaster, London, 1832, with open wicker-work wire sides and everted, naturalistic rim of cast vine decoration with grapes, tendrils and leaves.

Above right: Victorian ladle by Robert Garrard, 1853, with cast and chased handle in the form of bulrushes.

Louis Quatorze and Louis Quinze were names applied to styles taken from the eighteenth century. Rococo scrolls and floral motifs might be combined with ideas taken from French designs of that period, and it is almost impossible to distinguish one from the other. The classical Greek revival, during which inspiration was drawn at random from the whole gamut of Grecian or Etruscan design, appeared towards the middle of the century.

By the 1860s new designs were at last apparent. For several years various attempts had been made by designers to improve English design, but little attention was paid to them on the whole because the styles already described were so popular. Now at last these ideas began to receive attention. The International Exhibition of 1862 showed certain pieces which had been produced specially for the Exhibition by artists employing the new approach. At the conclusion of the Exhibition there was a general feeling that progress had been made in art over the decade or so since the Great Exhibition in 1851 with what was considered improvement in outlines and more attention to detail of workmanship. During the next ten years, while many of the flamboyant designs previously described were still produced, a new note of simplicity had

Victorian teapot from a three-piece tea set, London, 1847, decorated with shaded strapwork.

crept into the field of domestic silver. Angular shapes and styles began to appear, sometimes emphasised by appropriate decoration. Teapots, for instance, might have their rounded sides tapered down and outwards at quite a pronounced angle to a flat base, just before which they turned inwards at an opposing angle. Handles were taller than the body of the vessel and were usually straight across at the top.

Many people still preferred the established styles. A less emphatic form of naturalism as well as a pronounced version persisted concurrently with the popular Renaissance and classical designs, as well as those showing an Elizabethan or Moorish influence. The copies of late eighteenth century classical design apparent at the International Exhibition became exceedingly fashionable in the 1870s, and at this time also a new influence was felt which came from Japan. Displays of Japanese art had been on show in London since the 1860s, and had received much praise and acclaim, resulting in a general enthusiasm for Japanese design and decoration. During the 1870s Japanese-type engravings became fashionable on domestic silver, just as chinoiseries had been in vogue at the end of the seventeenth century and later. Japanese-inspired shapes also gradually appeared and by the 1880s were extremely fashionable. Handles might resemble bamboo, while engravings might include strange, exotic birds and Oriental plants. This infatuation with Japanese ideas even spread to the theatre where the first performance of Gilbert and Sullivan's *Mikado* was given in 1885.

The name Louis Seize was a term applied by the Victorians to copies of styles taken from the neo-classical period of the eighteenth century – a style also described as Adam, which was more to the point. The term 'Queen Anne' covered anything similar, or copies of shapes and decoration produced earlier in the eighteenth century as well as some later examples. The decoration which it embraced included strapwork, fluting, gadrooning and a general type of rococo.

A Liberty and Company lemonade jug, the tapering lobed body textured with hammer-finish and elongated, stylised flowers, Birmingham, 1900.

Emerging at this time was Art Nouveau, a brave new conception of design, derived from Japanese and mediæval art forms. Its unusual fluidity of line stimulated fresh interest in design. While manufacturers and retailers had no criticism of the above-mentioned hotchpotch of styles being produced and which sold very well, artists and designers of the period were becoming increasingly dismayed by the lack of originality and inspiration. Art Nouveau provided one answer. It was recognised at slightly different times from country to country but, as far as England was concerned, it began to make itself known around the last decade of the century, ending approximately with the advent of the First World War, although the first flush of enthusiasm for this style had lessened by about 1910. Unfortunately many of the early prototypes which were produced for silver were never actually made commercially, although by the turn of the twentieth century certain versions were being produced by Elkingtons, among other firms. Individual pieces were also made in the new style.

Among progressive designers was Charles Robert Ashbee (1863-1942), a trained architect, who for years had been a follower of William Morris (1834-1896), whose original thoughts and inspired designs had influenced many artist-craftsmen. By the 1880s this influence was becoming

apparent in silver, growing in its appeal until, in 1887, Ashbee founded
the School and Guild of Handicraft, the Guild finally discontinuing in
1908. Ashbee believed in the craftsman as opposed to mass-production
and commercially-made silver. Particularly during the first few years of
the Guild's existence, much beautiful silver was produced which bears
Ashbee's initials, since he was the chief designer. He trained the
craftsmen himself in hammering, raising, chasing and modelling and,
since none of these men had any previous experience of the craft, it must
be acknowledged that Ashbee did remarkably well in his brave venture.

Silver produced by the Guild was commonly undecorated, the surface
showing hammer marks. It was burnished to a soft, lustrous sheen, so
different from the hard metallic glint of commercially-made pieces.
Shapes, too, were very simple, based on the urn or pyriform outline
among others. Sugar casters might be cylindrical, resembling late
seventeenth century examples. Sugar bowls would have moulded edges
and wide wire handles, silver wire being a characteristic of Ashbee's
work, as were semi-precious stones and enamels. Ashbee used a stylised

Silver bowl, embossed
and chased with leaf
decoration, set upon
sinuous, cast legs,
designed by C. R. Ashbee
and made by the Guild of
Handicraft, *circa* 1893.

form of fine ornament, very much of his own stamp, with a Gothic feel about it, perhaps lobed and sometimes incorporating figures. Liberty and Company, which started business in 1875, greatly encouraged artist-designers, including those who produced Art Nouveau-inspired designs. They produced a range of designs in 1900 under the name of Cymric silver, characteristic of the work of contemporary designers, which also incorporated a Celtic or Art Nouveau influence.

Other guilds with similar objectives were formed by enthusiasts for the new cult, one such being the Birmingham Guild, founded by Arthur Dixon (1856-1929). The silver produced by this Guild was of a simple form, showing the hammer marks on the metal, and often undecorated. The designer W. A. S. Benson (1854-1924), although an admirer and follower of William Morris, tackled the problem of mass-production in a different way. His aim was to show that well-designed metalwork could be made on a commercial scale. He started to design and produce silver commercially in 1880 and seven years later opened his shop in Bond Street. Among his fine spun pieces was a silver-plated teapot, which was of a squat spherical shape with a large, looped handle covered in cane. Generally his pieces were in base metals. Sterling silver examples by Omar Ramsden (1873-1939) and Christopher Dresser (1834-1904) have become highly prized among collectors. Although Christopher Dresser designed silver wares as early as 1860, most examples of his work to be found today are much later, usually 1870 or 1880. His revolutionary silver and electro-plate is remarkable for its austere character, which was exceedingly progressive for the time and very functional. Many designs of the 1920s and 1930s would appear to have been greatly influenced by Christopher Dresser's work.

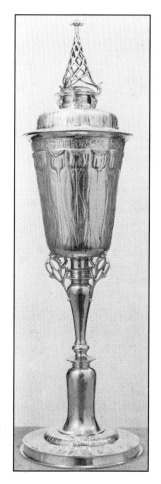

Silver and silver-gilt cup and cover, set with stones, by C. R. Ashbee, London, 1900.

4 Hallmarks

The subject of hallmarks is sometimes thought to be a complicated one, but this is not so. In fact, one of the greatest advantages of the system is its simplicity. What can confuse people is that much plated silver also has marks of one kind or another and these are sometimes taken for hallmarks. This has always been the case. It is why unscrupulous manufacturers of Sheffield plate gave their wares marks similar to those on sterling silver, until prohibited by law to do so. Likewise, a quick glance at marks on certain electro-plated goods may also mislead.

All sterling silver should be hallmarked, with a few exceptions which are mentioned later. Today there are only four Assay Offices in England – London, Birmingham, Sheffield and Edinburgh – but at one time there were many more. After 1 January 1975, these four Assay Offices started to use the same date letter, whereas previously each one used its own date letter, which changed annually. Thus in order to be able to date a piece it is necessary first to ascertain where it was assayed and then to consult lists of date letters for the respective Assay Office. All collectors of silver should know the mark for each Assay Office (termed the mark of origin), since it is highly likely that during the course of their collecting they will encounter pieces assayed at offices other than the four now in use.

London has occupied a place of unique importance since the Middle Ages. The mark of origin for London is a leopard's head (uncrowned from 1822), although this mark was first introduced in 1300 to show that the silver was of the required legal quality. There was one exception to this – it was replaced by the lion's head erased between 1697 and 1720, during which time the Britannia standard was enforced.

Above, left to right: the leopard's head crowned, the mark of origin for London; the leopard's head uncrowned, the mark of origin for London from 1822; the lion's head erased, the mark which was used instead of the leopard's head on London silver during the Britannia period.

Only 63 years after King Edward I had passed the Statute decreeing that the leopard's head should be used, a further Ordinance ordered that 'each Master Goldsmith should have a mark to himself . . . and after the assay has taken place, the supervisors shall put on the King's mark (the leopard's head), and then the goldsmith his mark'. Thus two marks now appeared on all sterling silver.

When the leopard's head was introduced in 1300, it was specified that 'in all the good towns of England, where there are goldsmiths . . . one shall go from each town for all the others to London to seek their sure touch'. Therefore all silver produced in England at that time usually bears the London leopard's head, although it need not have been made in London. As other Assay Offices came into being, goldsmiths would select the nearest one and travel there with their wares to receive the necessary marks. It follows, therefore, that the mark of origin does not necessarily mean that the piece was made in that town, merely that this is where it was assayed.

The introduction of a third stamp, the annual date letter, was enforced in 1478. A 20-letter cycle was adopted omitting J and ending at U (also shaped like a V), and the date letter was changed each year on 19 May, St Dunstan's Day, the form of the letter or its shield also altering with each new alphabet. Occasionally the shape might be changed during the course of the year to show a change of assayer.

A date letter: this shows in which year the piece was assayed.

Even before 1300 efforts were made in London to regularise the standard of silver. A decree of 1238 instructed the mayor and aldermen to choose six of the more discreet goldsmiths of the City to superintend the craft, to see that certain standards were maintained, and to ensure that silver should not be of a worse fineness than that used for the coinage. Gradually the responsibilities of the goldsmiths became more specified. The Act of 1300 also added that 'no goldsmith of England, nor none other where within the King's dominion . . . shall from henceforth make or cause to be made any manner of vessel, jewel or any other thing of gold or silver, except it be of good and true alloy, that is to say, gold of a certain touch, and silver of the sterling alloy' (see chapter 2). Twenty-seven years later, Edward III granted a royal charter to 'the Wardens and Commonalty of the Mystery of Goldsmiths of the City of London' (ie mystery meaning trade or craft). The London Goldsmiths' Company later built a hall in the City where their assaying was carried out, and from which derives the term hallmarking.

Although there is no official record to account for the addition of a fourth mark in 1544, it is thought to have resulted from the debasement of the currency begun in 1542 by Henry VIII, and the fact that the public needed to be reassured over the standard of silver used in wares. The mark took the form of a lion passant guardant. It has been recorded that the King was much displeased with the Goldsmiths' Company, which was instructed to surrender its charter and privileges. His death, three years after the introduction of the lion passant guardant, is thought to have saved the Company.

The lion passant guardant: the mark which proves that the piece is of sterling silver, 925 parts of pure silver.

Britannia silver – *not* Britannia metal which is an alloy of tin, antimony and copper resembling silver – is the term used for silver of a higher standard, produced between 1697 and 1720. During this time the standard was raised from 925 fine to 958 fine. The reason for this unprecedented measure was that the demand for silver wares exceeded the amount of bullion available at that time, and goldsmiths were in the practice of accepting parcels of silver from anywhere, included in which might be melted-down coins or plate. This encouraged the harmful practice of coin clipping, resulting in a general erosion of confidence in the currency. Easy to understand when, according to records, a coin might be deprived of up to one-fifth of its correct weight. By raising the standard legally required for silver wares, therefore, thus differentiating between the standard for currency and that for goods, this easy conversion from coins to silverware was stopped.

The new Britannia standard did not apply to either Scottish or Irish silver. While it was in force the Britannia mark (a seated figure of Britannia) was used as was a lion's head erased, which replaced the lion passant guardant and the crowned leopard's head. The maker's mark, as laid down by the Act, was to consist of the first two letters of the maker's surname. After June 1720, when the Statute for the termination of the higher standard came into force, the old sterling standard was restored, although goldsmiths were permitted to make wares of the Britannia standard if they preferred. In 1738, another Statute commanded goldsmiths to destroy their former marks and register new ones which were to consist of initials only and of a different style of lettering to previous examples.

The mark of Britannia: the mark which shows that the silver is of a higher quality, 958 parts of pure silver.

In 1784 an Act re-imposed a duty of sixpence ($2\frac{1}{2}$p) on each ounce of silver made, and as a receipt or acknowledgement of the duty, the silver was given another hallmark: that of the sovereign's head. This was enforced until 1890. Certain small pieces of silver which were already exempt from hallmarking were not included in the re-imposed duty. These had been exempted in the Plate Offences Act of 1738 and included chains, lockets, buttons, thimbles, coral sockets and bells, pipelighters, small nutmeg graters, sliding pencils, small cases and similar items. In 1790, the Plate Offences Acts of 1738 and 1784 were amended and chains, necklace beads, lockets, filigree work, shirt buckles or brooches, stamped medals and most objects weighing less than five pennyweights were exempted. However, the necks, collars and tops of casters, cruets or glasses were not.

The sovereign's head: this proves that duty was paid on the silver.

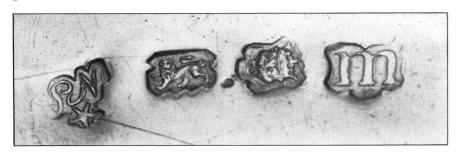

Close-up of London hallmarks: NS (the maker's mark, Nicholas Sprimont); the lion passant guardant (denoting that the piece is of sterling silver); the leopard's head (London mark); and the date letter m (1747).

Provincial Assay Offices

Provincial Assay Offices included Bristol, Chester, Exeter, Newcastle, Norwich, York and later Birmingham and Sheffield. Scotland and Ireland are dealt with separately later in this chapter.

Bristol

The Statute of 1700 set up Assay Offices in towns where there were mints: York, Exeter, Bristol, Chester and Norwich, and records kept by Isaac Newton, Master of the Mint at Bristol until his death in 1727, show that there was an Assay Master at Bristol. The Statute enforced such matters as the election of Wardens, the appointment of a skilled assayer and the keeping of a Diet Box. A portion of the scrapings taken from each article was to be left in this and tested annually by the Royal Mint as a check on the accuracy of provincial assays. It is assumed that the Bristol Assay Office was active between 1720 and 1740, generally indicated by marks found on specific pieces of silver. The mark of origin for Bristol was a ship issuing from a castle, but an earlier mark is thought to have been a BR in monogram. Bristol firms later sent their wares to Exeter to be marked, where by 1865 it is estimated that over 60 per cent of the silver assayed at the Exeter Assay Office was made in Bristol.

Chester

Moneyers were working at Chester from Saxon days, and the Domesday Book refers to Mint Masters of the town. However, no reference to Chester appears in the usual early Acts, possibly because the town came under the jurisdiction of the Earl of Chester and not the Crown until the days of Henry VIII. In 1686-87, the goldsmiths of Chester met and drew up a statement of intent which cited all legislation concerning the standards of gold and silver from the year 1300. The Wardens' marks were to be the coat-of-arms and crest of the City of Chester on two individual punches, the crest being a sheathed sword, point uppermost, and belt attached, resting on an orle. The coat-of-arms of the city was a sword erect between three wheat sheaves. The date letter series started in 1687 with a capital A, which was not changed each year. It was altered to B on 2 June 1690 and C in April 1692, and from then on approximately every two years, finally concluding in 1697.

Mark of origin for Chester.

In 1700 a new Assay Office came into being and the town mark incorporated was the newer version of the city arms: three demi-lions passant and one-and-a-half wheat sheaves. This was used until 1777, after which time the ancient arms of the city were re-introduced, and used until the office closed in 1962. Following the reinstatement of the original sterling standard, the date letter and the lion passant guardant, together with the town mark, were joined by the leopard's head crowned. From 1823 the crown was removed and from 1838 the leopard's head was discontinued.

Exeter

An Assay Office was opened in Exeter in 1700, though goldsmiths had worked there for centuries, and they were officially incorporated into a Company at the same time. The town mark was the triple-towered castle from the city's coat-of-arms, used with a date letter alphabet of 24 letters (omitting J and U), changed annually on 7 August. The new standard marks of a lion's head erased and a figure of Britannia were used until the re-introduction of the old sterling standard in 1720, when Exeter adopted the crowned leopard's head in addition to its own town mark. The leopard's head crowned was no longer used after 1777 and the office closed in 1883.

Mark of origin for Exeter.

Newcastle

The Goldsmiths' Company of Newcastle first met in 1702 and a new Assay Office was also inaugurated, though goldsmiths had been working there from approximately the middle of the thirteenth century. The town mark, taken from the city arms, consisted of three towers. A variable series of date letters was used, as was the lion's head erased and the figure of Britannia. With the return of the old sterling standard in 1720, the leopard's head became an additional mark. The office closed in 1884.

Mark of origin for Newcastle.

Norwich

Norwich became a working assay town in the second half of the sixteenth century. Date letters reappeared in 1688 and continued until 1697, but only a small quantity of silver was assayed there after 1701 and the office was closed shortly afterwards. Marks for Norwich include: the castle over a lion, a separate crown and a rose, and a crowned rose. The maker's mark was also punched.

York

York was the second most important city in England during the Middle Ages, and the goldsmiths there had their own touch mark and a town mark as early as 1411. The fifteenth century mark was half a leopard's head with half a fleur-de-lys, conjoined in a circular punch. In 1701 this was changed to five lions passant on a cross and from 1778 this was enclosed in a shield until nine years later, when an oval replaced the shield. Date letters were used from the sixteenth century. The office was closed in 1858.

Mark of origin for York.

Birmingham and Sheffield

Both the Birmingham and the Sheffield Assay Offices were established far later than other provincial offices and for the same reason. More efficient mechanism combined with technological progress, the use of harder steels and the very thin silver rolled to a finer gauge by the latest mills, all contributed towards cutting costs to such an extent that there was an enormous rise in the demand for domestic silver. Goldsmiths in Birmingham and Sheffield were tired of conveying their wares to their nearest Assay Offices to be marked, for this meant a journey to Chester in the case of Birmingham, and Chester or York in the case of Sheffield; London was another alternative. Matthew Boulton, a well-established and influential Birmingham manufacturer of metal goods and the son of a prosperous button and buckle manufacturer, determined that an Assay Office should be opened in Birmingham and sought the support of local tradespeople and influential gentry.

The Sheffield Cutlers' Company learnt of his attempts and in 1772 Boulton received a letter from their clerk asking to be included in his plans so that the two towns could unite in a petition to Parliament. As a result of a Parliamentary Committee's Enquiry in 1773 and the petition, an Act for appointing Wardens and Assay Masters for assaying wrought plate in the towns of Sheffield and Birmingham was passed in 1773. The Act also prohibited the stamping of any letters upon any manufactured article of metal plated, or covered with, or looking like silver. It was modified in 1784 and allowed manufacturers of plated goods within 100 miles of Sheffield to strike their surnames or the name of their partnership with some device alongside, but these were not to bear any similarity to a hallmark, and were to be registered at the Assay Office.

The chosen town mark for Birmingham was an anchor (struck either vertically or horizontally), and a crown for Sheffield. The latter under the Statute of 1973 was replaced by a rose. The Birmingham Assay Office started by using an alphabet of 25 date letters – omitting J – which was changed every year in July. The succeeding alphabet which started in 1798 used all 26 letters. The next, starting in 1824, consisted of 25 letters, then 26 for the one begun in 1849. From 1875 each successive

Above, left to right: the anchor: mark of origin for Birmingham; the crown: mark of origin for Sheffield; the rose: mark of origin for Sheffield from 1975.

alphabet has been of 25 letters. The bicentenary of the office was celebrated in 1973 by the use of a special mark in that year: the anchor with a small letter c on either side of it.

Sheffield used a selection of random letters of the alphabet as date letters until 1824. By 1868 a 25-letter cycle had been developed. From 1780 to 1853 a combined punch of the crown and date letter was usual. For five years between 1815 and 1820 the crown mark was struck upside down to the date letter. In common with the Birmingham office, the sovereign's head duty mark was struck twice in 1797 to show that double duty was paid.

Scottish silver

Scottish marks are known as early as the middle of the fifteenth century. By 1681 the goldsmiths of Edinburgh had adopted a variable date letter and abandoned the deacon's mark instituted in 1457 for the mark of the Assay Master. This in its turn was substituted by a thistle in 1759. The town mark is a triple-towered castle.

Close-up of Edinburgh hallmarks: L & R (the makers' mark, Lothian and Robertson); the date letter E (1759); the thistle; and the triple-towered castle of Edinburgh.

Although there was an active group of goldsmiths in Glasgow, mentioned in records as early as 1536, no Glasgow silver earlier than approximately 1681 appears to be marked with anything but perhaps the maker's mark and burgh arms: a tree with a bird on the top, a hand bell suspended from the branches and across or below the trunk a salmon with a ring in its mouth (termed the fish, tree and bell mark). A date letter also came into use but was discontinued after 1710. It was regularised in 1819, and was used until the office closed in 1964. From about 1730 to approximately 1800 the letter S, in a shaped punch which was varied, was also generally applied and is thought to represent 'Sterling' or 'Standard Quality'. The marks for Glasgow, after an Act of 1819 which constituted the Glasgow Goldsmiths' Company a body corporate, were the date letter, the lion rampant mark – from the Royal Standard of Scotland – used as the standard mark, the town mark, maker's mark and sovereign's duty mark.

Mark of origin for Glasgow.

Apart from Edinburgh and Glasgow there were various other towns where silver was marked including Canongate (now part of Edinburgh), Aberdeen, Arbroath, Dundee, Elgin, Greenock, Inverness, Montrose, Perth, Tain and Wick.

In Scotland, although the sovereign's head was struck on silver after 1784 – in common with England – to indicate that duty had been paid, there was sometimes a delay in the change of the head following the accession of a new monarch. The head of Queen Victoria, for instance, did not appear on Edinburgh silver until some four years after she had become queen.

Irish silver

Irish silver, often hard to date, was not marked until the seventeenth century, although silversmiths had worked in Ireland from early times. A Royal Charter was granted by Charles I to Dublin goldsmiths in 1637, ordaining that their silver was to be marked by the harp crowned – the

King's Majesty's stamp and the standard of fineness – and the maker's mark. A date letter was used irregularly from 1638. The mark of Hibernia was added in 1730-31. Note should be made that the figure of Hibernia can be particularly misleading for beginners, since it can be easily confused with the Britannia mark. Approximately ten years after the disuse of Britannia, the Irish Parliament taxed certain items of silver to raise funds for agricultural improvements. To show that payment had been received, the mark of Hibernia was stamped. The head of the sovereign – the duty mark used in England – was stamped from 1807 to 1890, replacing that of Hibernia as a duty mark, and Hibernia, retained, became the town mark of Dublin.

The assaying of Dublin silver was not always consistent, some being sold unmarked and other pieces bearing only the crowned harp, Hibernia and a maker's mark. This applies to the period covered by the reigns of George II and George III and, since the year letter was omitted there is no possibility of dating pieces by this method. Until approximately 1850 the maker's mark generally consisted of the initials of Christian and surname, separate or monogrammed, and could be crowned or used in conjunction with an emblem until about 1760. During the nineteenth century the complete surname sometimes appeared. Silver assayed at Dublin was usually of good quality and often of fine workmanship. Emigré Huguenot silversmiths sought refuge in Ireland after the Revocation of the Edict of Nantes in 1685 and their fine work influenced the general standard.

Although the law required Irish silversmiths to have their wares assayed in Dublin, this edict was often ignored. Silversmiths sometimes preferred to avoid payment of the duty which was required from 1730 and thus their wares would be marked inconsistently, perhaps with unfamiliar devices. Among those who disregarded the law were the silversmiths of Cork, who belonged to the Company of the Society of Goldsmiths of the City of Cork, a body which admitted other craftsmen and tradesmen into its ranks. The town mark until 1715 was a ship in full sail between two castles, all details of which might appear in one punch, but sometimes the ship might be alone in a punch with the castle being punched once – or twice – separately. Cork silver after 1710 might also be marked Sterling, and this also appeared sometimes on Galway silver between 1650 and 1730. Silversmiths were also known to have worked at Limerick, Youghal, Kinsale, Londonderry and Kilkenny.

Top: the Dublin standard of fineness mark.

Above: Hibernia, the stamp originally used to show that Irish duty had been paid.

Fakes and forgeries

Despite the fact that the English hallmarking system is ancient and well-tested (see chapter 2), it cannot be relied upon purely for the authenticity of a piece. Its very reputation, respected and revered the world over, makes it vulnerable to dishonest use by fakers and forgers. Transposing marks from one object to another is not an uncommon practice and can be very lucrative when the piece is sold for a high price. Genuine marks may also be removed from an older, damaged object and 'married' to a far later example. This is why experts will sometimes breathe on a piece for, by doing so, the outline of the joins which are invisible to the naked eye should reveal themselves. Certainly when the object is oxidised the let-in silver usually shows fairly clearly. This practice of transposition is not a new one and has been used for many years.

There are various other types of faking. Britannia silver (earlier described in this chapter) is of a higher standard and is more costly, and such pieces are therefore always in demand. An encouraging thought for the faker. Britannia standard silver is still produced legitimately today as an alternative to the sterling standard available to silversmiths since 1720. Such objects will be punched with the much-prized Britannia mark. Assuming that the object upon which it is punched is in the appropriate style of similar, earlier pieces, all that is needed is a mechanical buffer to slightly wear down the marks which by now would have worn with time and usage, leaving sufficient of the Britannia outline to interest the collector, and the object is ready to fetch a high price.

Another trick, and perhaps an even more insidious one, is to remove the marks on the base of a damaged or less important item and 'marry' it to a later piece. This can be convincing. Should any vessel which you are planning to buy such as a teapot, tankard, coffee pot, etc, have a lid, therefore, it is always wise to check the hallmarks on both the base and the lid to make sure that they agree. The forger by his very nature is a gambler and will trust to luck that not everybody will check all marks.

There are as well far more skilled and overwhelming fakes involving the complete transformation of objects. Perhaps you may never come into contact with any of these, but no piece is really safe. An unfashionable vessel, perhaps a goblet, can be quite simply transformed into a desirable pierced sugar bowl, complete with blue-glass liner. Mugs can be transformed into delightful jugs. Unobtrusive repairs or additions may restore a piece to its previous visual attraction, and then the unscrupulous dealer may ask the original price. Sometimes this is justified; sometimes it is not. I once observed a customer in the shop of an Amsterdam purveyor of old silver about to buy a delightful mid-eighteenth century English silver milk jug. It was a charming, pear-shaped jug and stood upon three delicate hoof feet: none of which matched. A damaged spoon with a sought-after trifid end, bearing late seventeenth century hallmarks, can be transformed with certain judicious hammering and cutting, into a three-pronged fork. Mote skimmers can be converted from tea spoons and few will notice that they are not quite the right length. The permutations are endless.

The Goldsmiths' Company organise various exhibitions at Goldsmiths' Hall, Foster Lane, London, EC2 from time to time. Among these was one devoted to 500 years of hallmarking, which included some very interesting examples of the practices of the faker and forger. A pewter jug *circa* 1826, with maker's mark RM, was complete with pseudo-hallmarks of a dagger, leopard's head and cockerel. Pewterers commonly marked their wares with simulated hallmarks. An electro-plated late nineteenth century ladle also bore a convincing set of mock hallmarks. Three trifid spoons had been cast from a seventeenth century original, complete with cast hallmarks, these being detectable by the expert because the random striking of each mark would never have been identically spaced on each spoon. Early eighteenth century forks had been made from spoons of a later period because they would fetch higher prices. A small, bachelor teapot, *circa* 1808, had been converted from a sugar basin by the addition of a handle, spout and lid. A mustard pot had been given a set of fake marks for the year 1820, detectable because fake punches were often made of lower quality steel to those used by Assay Offices, and give a 'softer' impression.

Knowing the right place to look for marks can sometimes be of help in detecting dishonesty. Early examples of teapots, coffee pots and chocolate pots, for example, usually have their marks punched in a line beneath the rim at the top of the vessel, close to the handle. From approximately 1760 this practice changed and the marks generally were stamped on the base. But as with all objects which have additional pieces, the lids should also be marked, although not necessarily with a full set of marks. Very early spoons were usually marked inside their bowls, generally close to the stem. When the addition of the maker's mark became law, this was punched at the back of the stem as was the date letter. The lion passant guardant also found his way there. The mark of origin stayed in the bowl until towards the final decades of the seventeenth century when it became the custom for it to be struck on the stem next to the maker's mark. It was not unusual for mid-eighteenth century tea spoons to bear only the mark of the lion passant, but from about this time onwards marks are usually complete.

As with spoons, sugar tongs may have either a full set of marks, or certain marks only, perhaps the lion passant or date letter, more usually found with earlier examples than those made towards and after the nineteenth century. Breakages can also account for the lack of certain marks, which may be obliterated during repair work. London hallmarks during the nineteenth century were made in sizes ranging in height from one-quarter-of-an-inch (6mm), to one-sixteenth-of-an-inch (1.5mm) in the case of small marks. The punches were placed in a frame which kept them in strict alignment, so that they could be stamped quickly. This can help to detect a reproduction of an earlier shape which has mellowed over the years.

5 Sheffield Plate

Sheffield plate has grown considerably in popularity among collectors, and prices can, therefore, be high. Nevertheless, when bought with care it is a good proposition for both its beauty and usually its value as an investment. Although it is plated silver its attraction lies in the softness of its tone and generally the standard of craftsmanship is good, with the exception of certain later types of Sheffield plate and cheap imported plate, with which this book is not concerned since it is devoted to English-made wares. Sadly, the man who discovered the technique of Sheffield plate failed to grasp its full potential. Others were quick to do so, however, and for about 100 years between its appearance and its replacement by electro-plate in the following century, an enormous number and variety of wares was produced by this method.

A Sheffield cutler, Thomas Boulsover, discovered in about 1742 that a sheet of silver could be fused by heat onto a thicker piece of copper. The metals, thus fused as one, were then rolled from the ingot into a thin sheet of copper coated with a layer of silver. Thomas Boulsover used his new plated copper for making small objects, particularly buttons and boxes. From approximately the mid-1750s, Joseph Hancock, a former apprentice to Boulsover, started to make miscellaneous domestic articles with the new silver-coated plate and in 1762 acquired Thomas Boulsover's works.

The new process was not known as Sheffield plate until around 1770. It had been virtually an instant success because of its lower cost, and when in 1784 a tax of sixpence ($2\frac{1}{2}$p) an ounce was re-imposed on sterling silver, its popularity increased further since the price of Sheffield plate was around one-third of that for silver. Sheffield plate did not long remain the sole product of Sheffield. Matthew Boulton, an astute and energetic manufacturer of metal goods in Birmingham, visited Sheffield to learn the techniques of the new process and in 1762 began production of Sheffield plate at his Soho, Birmingham, workshop. He quickly obtained a monopoly on its manufacture in Birmingham, and became the largest manufacturer of Sheffield plate. After about eight years other manufacturers set up production and by the end of the century their numbers had grown considerably. Matthew Boulton's wares were made to a very high standard, but he was not alone in striving for quality. Sheffield plate manufacturers generally worked hard to produce wares of a good standard, even though the very nature of the silver-plated copper often made this difficult. Although by the following century Birmingham had strengthened its position and had practically ousted Sheffield from

Sheffield plate soup tureen in the shape of a turtle, *circa* 1800, length 22 inches.

the market by the 1830s, Birmingham products on the whole – with the exception of Matthew Boulton's fine wares – were generally cheaper than those made in Sheffield.

Vessels made of very early Sheffield plate and all other objects were produced from copper plated only on one side with silver, and were tinned inside where necessary. After about the mid-1760s new methods made it possible to coat the copper with silver on both sides which resulted in the plate becoming practically indistinguishable from silver, particularly since the silver used by Sheffield platers was of sterling quality (925 fine) and not pure silver as was used later by electro-platers. Once the plate had been rolled to the right gauge by passing it repeatedly between pressure rollers it was ready to be made into wares and the methods employed were usually the same as for sterling silver wares (see chapter 2). The craftsmen who hand-raised Sheffield plate were known as braziers, who worked in the old ways of the silversmith, shaping hollow-wares on a steel stake, hammering them into their various forms by striking repeatedly with a mallet, then burnishing and decorating. Certain wares would be formed by folding the metal around and joining at the seam, a circular base then being soldered into place. From approximately 1820, hollow-ware was shaped by lathe-spinning and pieces produced by this method can sometimes be detected with the traces of the spiralling pressure in their interiors.

The soft hue of Sheffield plate which delights collectors today is often enhanced by a charming reddish tinge where the coating of silver has worn over the years to reveal the copper beneath. However, since Sheffield plate was intended to simulate the exact shade of silver, such attributes would hardly have excited its manufacturers who tried painstakingly hard to eliminate such deficiences. A problem which plagued them was the appearance of the copper along the edges where the plate had been cut, but eventually it was possible to plate copper wire and use it to conceal these telltale edges. Sterling silver wire was also used for the same purpose, and the edges of Matthew Boulton's wares of sterling silver (Birmingham) were marked with the words Silver Borders, while Sheffield manufacturers used the wording Silver Edged, sometimes omitting the final e or d. Sterling silver was also later used as shields and mounts. It was not possible to engrave ordinary Sheffield plate with a graver, which would cut away the silver to reveal the copper beneath. A technique of rubbing-in silver shields was discovered in approximately 1810, and prior to this time such shields were soldered into position.

Eventually the many problems which the reddish colour of the copper had always caused were completely solved by another plating process. In 1830 Samuel Roberts took out a patent which further concealed the copper by using a layer of German silver (nickel silver) between the sterling silver and the copper. German silver contained no silver and is a misnomer. Thus when the sterling silver became worn the German 'silver' was revealed instead of the copper. Costs were cut by the new process since less sterling silver was needed than when fused straight onto copper. German silver was an alloy of copper, zinc and nickel, the proportions of which varied depending on its uses. Birmingham and Sheffield plate manufacturers imported it in ingots, mostly from Germany. It was a hard alloy, too brittle at first to be used to replace copper entirely, but after about six years the alloy had been sufficiently improved to replace copper altogether. The term British plate is used to describe the plate resulting from a fusion of sterling silver with the new, less brittle alloy, in which diverse wares were made from about 1836.

Sheffield plate tea spoon, *circa* 1790.

It was not unusual for manufacturers of plated silver to stamp their products with marks very similar to silver hallmarks, and these have deceived many people over the years – especially new collectors (see chapter 4). In some cases the marks have been cunningly designed to look very similar to legitimate hallmarks and only upon close inspection do their discrepancies gradually become apparent. Some pieces of early Sheffield plate are marked with distinguishing marks, but it was illegal to mark Sheffield plate between 1773 and 1784 because of the growing similarity to hallmarks. After this date Sheffield plate manufacturers were authorised to mark their wares with an emblem plus the maker's name, but in no way were the marks to simulate silver hallmarks. Certain manufacturers ignored this directive and returned to marking their wares in such a way that they might be mistaken for silver, while others did not mark their wares at all. It is therefore virtually impossible to specifically date or identify much Sheffield plate. Fines were imposed for the apathy in the latter case but seemed to have little effect.

Sheffield plate inkstand
with two glass bottles:
one for ink and the other
for sand, with a wafer
box in the centre.
Maker's mark D. Holy,
Parker and Company,
circa 1804.

Registration of marks for plated goods virtually ceased after 1836 because the new British plate could not correctly be termed Sheffield plate as silver was not fused onto copper. Yet again manufacturers resorted to marking their wares with unregistered symbols which looked very much like hallmarks. After 1765, and more so following the turn of the nineteenth century, a crown was sometimes used in addition to other marks. This was originally intended to show that the piece was of good quality, and its use grew at the conclusion of the Napoleonic wars in 1815 to differentiate between English plate and cheap wares imported from France. Manufacturers used it increasingly throughout the nineteenth century until the public were in such a state of confusion, since it was also the mark for the Sheffield Assay Office, that its use was eventually prohibited in 1896.

Apart from bogus marks, collectors should also watch out for another ploy which manufacturers used. It is illegal to describe wares as being made of Sheffield plate if they have not been produced by the correct method, ie fusing silver to copper. Later manufacturers often described pieces electro-plated on copper as Sheffield plated, adding the 'd' to keep within the confines of the law. To add to the confusion, certain registered marks of Sheffield plate manufacturers have also been used on electro-plating, including symbols used consistently by *bona fide* manufacturers of Sheffield plate. Among others these included the bell, the hand, the crossed arrows, the pineapple and the crossed keys.

Sadly there appears to be no record of a mark used by the originator of Sheffield plate, Thomas Boulsover, but there is certainly one for Joseph Hancock *circa* 1755. His initials are punched in a similar way to those used by London silversmiths of the period. Other marks for the 1750s, 1760s and 1770s include the initials of the following manufacturers: Nathaniel Smith; Thomas Law; Tudor and Leader; John Hoyland and Company; Boulton and Fothergill; Jacob and Samuel Roberts; John Winter and Company; J. Rowbotham and Company; Ashforth, Ellis and Company; and J. Littlewood. Where the initial J is used it generally looks like a capital I.

Sheffield plate knitting sheath, *circa* 1770. The sheath was attached to the waist.

Many and varied were the emblems used by Sheffield plate manufacturers after 1784 when a device had to accompany the name. Eighteenth century symbols included: two keys crossed (1784, John Parsons and Company); the palm of a hand (1784, N. Smith and Company); a triangle upon a triangle (1785, Deakin, Smith and Company); crossbow (1789, W. Jervis); a squirrel (1794, E. Goodwin); and a ram's head (1797, Froggatt, Coldwell and Lean). For further marks and information see the standard book on old Sheffield plate, *History of Old Silver Plate* by Frederick Bradbury, and the same author's invaluable pocket-sized *Book of Hallmarks*, which incorporates old Sheffield plate marks.

Marks apart, there are other ways of differentiating between Sheffield plate and a bogus imitation. The most important characteristic is the colour of Sheffield plate. In a good, natural light it has a soft bluish tinge, quite dissimilar to the later types of plate when silver was fused onto German silver, or the harder colour of electro-plate. Next, look out for seams. These should be detectable on the type of wares which would have been made by joining at a seam. If they are not apparent you can generally assume that the piece was electro-plated, either as an original electro-plated piece, or as a re-plated object. This practice was common during the final decades of the nineteenth century, when many fine old pieces of Sheffield plate which were becoming worn were sent off for an electro-plated 'face-lift'. Where this has occurred, of course, collectors should pass over the object. Hinges can be important on old Sheffield plate. They usually warrant a close inspection since, after the considerable use these have received over the years, some wear and tear is reasonable. Hinges on reproductions will gleam like the rest of the object, showing no wear.

A knowledge of the type of decoration used at various periods can greatly assist the collector. Ornament usually followed the cyclic fashions set by London silversmiths who continued to use hand-craftsmen for many years after factory methods became more general. Later, ornamental patterns were produced by the factories themselves in Sheffield and Birmingham. Engraving and bright-cutting, two very popular forms of late eighteenth century decoration, presented immediate problems when carried out on Sheffield plate because the cut-away metal revealed the glow of the copper. Yet because bright-cutting had become so fashionable on neo-classical domestic wares, it was essential that Sheffield plate manufacturers found some way of resolving the problem. At first they bright-cut bands of silver which were soldered onto the Sheffield plate, but by using a deeper layer of silver on the copper it was also possible to bright-cut directly onto the Sheffield plate.

Piercing, which had been popular on silver wares since the early eighteenth century, was impossible to execute in the same way craftsmen produced pierced sterling silver wares. Early examples of sterling silver were cut with a fret-saw, and once again this technique would have revealed the copper on Sheffield plate. For this reason early Sheffield plate is not pierced. The earliest examples of pierced Sheffield plate date from around the final years of the 1760s when hand-operated fly-presses were equipped with steel tools which, with their hard and

specially-shaped ends, were used to pierce the perforations. The tool was
designed in such a way as to pull the layered silver from the plate,
causing it to project past the copper. In this way the silver could be turned
down to hide the red of the copper. Each shaped perforation was pressed
by hand individually to begin with but by the last decade or so of the
eighteenth century, the holes were pressed in numbers which speeded up
the work considerably. Within the next 20 years from about 1820
steam-operated presses became general.

Above left: Sheffield plate
salt cellar, *circa* 1790.

Above right: Sheffield
plate teapot, *circa* 1821.

Embossing presented few problems since no metal is cut away with this
technique. Embossing in high-relief necessitated the use of plate which
had been fused with a deeper layer of silver, in case the silver flaked
during working and the copper was revealed. As with silver, embossing
was particularly popular until approximately the last quarter of the
eighteenth century, reappearing again in the nineteenth century
according to the dictates of fashion. A great many domestic vessels were
decorated by embossing, including tea and coffee services. In 1822
further mechanisation, in the form of a press which simulated
hand-chasing, was used for ornament on trays and similar flat objects. In
a single operation this could impress flowers, scrolls or other shapes on
the plate. Flat chasing was much apparent on Sheffield plate from the
final two decades of the eighteenth century, often in conjunction with
piercing. It adorned most domestic wares including mustard pots,
coasters, salt cellars, muffineers, tea caddies, sugar bowls, teapots and
coffee pots. Fluting and reeding were common, although on earlier
examples the indentations are less pronounced. These two forms of
decoration are also found on certain Sheffield plate made during the first
few years or so of the nineteenth century.

Gilding (see chapter 2) was essential for the interiors of certain vessels
which did not contain glass linings, for it prevented corrosion or staining.
Thus this can be found in salt cellars, cream jugs, mustard pots, etc,
although quite large vessels such as punch bowls might also have their
interiors gilded. Certain hollow-wares, including tea urns, hot-water

Sheffield plate coffee pot
with the mark of Daniel
Holy and Company, *circa*
1825.

jugs, teapots, coffee pots and others, had their interiors tinned, a method
which was used as late as the 1820s for, among others, flat items such as
trays. Tinning conjures up a vision of cheapness, yet, in fact, it had a
pleasant appearance. It was highly polished before it left the factory and
at a quick glance was not dissimilar to silver. Although the layer of tin
was generally quite thick, most pieces in constant use needed to be
re-tinned occasionally.

From approximately the earlier years of the 1770s separate parts of a
vessel such as spouts or lids were stamped out using a drop-hammer. The
piece of Sheffield plate would be placed upon a striking block which had a
die sunk with a model of the required shape. Then the hammer, the face
of which was raised with the same shape as the sunken die, was
manipulated from above by a rope between two vertical rods and, as it
struck the block, the Sheffield plate was stamped into shape. The parts
would then be soldered to the vessel. The introduction of harder steels
made possible more sharply-defined pieces and during the Regency period
entire units were produced in this manner. Die-stamping was a very
important technique, advances in it contributing greatly to
mass-production methods in both silver and Sheffield plate. By the last
decade of the eighteenth century larger, flat pieces such as trays were
being produced in this manner, suitably ornamented as already
described.

Die-stamping had thus become of considerable importance to the silversmith and Sheffield plate manufacturer, both of whom increasingly relied upon it to keep down prices for an ever-expanding market. In particular this technique was used for candlesticks and, since a complete set of candlestick dies was an expensive investment, these were not uncommonly hired to manufacturers which meant that identical specimens were produced by different makers, hence these may bear different marks even though they are of the same shape and decoration. Candlestick manufacture was one of the most lucrative and important branches of the Sheffield plate industry, and the range and assortment of designs was vast. Platers sometimes made nothing else, their products being elegant yet realistically priced. Small wonder, then, that their products were so much in demand. Pattern books at the Victoria and Albert Museum reveal that during the last decade or so of the eighteenth century the price for a pair of 12-inch candlesticks was around 40 shillings (£2).

Candlesticks were commonly made in six parts: pedestal and foot, tubular stem or pillar, inner tube of the pillar, candle socket, hoop (a tube affixed to the pan to secure the nozzle) and nozzle. These sections were joined by solder after any rough edges had been filed, the tubular stem being vertically seamed. Ornamentation would have been die-struck on the metal when it was flat, although hand-finishing in the form of chasing was also used in conjunction with it. Neo-classical table candlesticks followed the fashion set by sterling silver versions and were invariably derived from ancient classical architecture including Tuscan and Doric pillars and Corinthian columns. Decorations including rams' heads, floral swags or bows might be found around the foot or below the socket. Although Sheffield plate candlesticks, and other domestic items, followed contemporary fashions, they sometimes lagged behind high fashion, since it was costly to change dies until sales really declined and demand for them had ceased. After the first few years of the nineteenth century, approximately between 1815 and the 1830s, it became expedient and profitable to stamp the parts of candlesticks in wafer-thin metal and to strengthen and weight them with an inexpensive alloy. Certain sterling silver examples might have various parts such as inner tubes, nozzles and pans made of Sheffield plate, while some candlesticks were not hallmarked because the silver did not come up to the required standard. In addition, many sub-standard candlesticks were produced during the Napoleonic wars because Sheffield plate was rolled to a very thin gauge owing to the diminishing supply of silver and copper.

Candelabra had become increasingly popular and were made in Sheffield plate throughout the eighteenth and into the nineteenth century. It was also possible to transform a candlestick into its more elaborate relative by purchasing branches which were available for this purpose, as were their sterling silver counterparts. Conversely, the branches on actual candelabra were removable so that the pillar could be used as a candlestick. Most earlier branches were of a plain appearance with recurving arms coming from the bottom of the finial. They needed to be strengthened and usually this was done by filling them with soft solder. Twin branches were generally more favoured than three or four, although up to seven candle holders appeared on some more complicated

Sheffield plate candlestick, *circa* 1780.

versions. Candelabra of this type might reach 36 inches in height, but during the eighteenth century the usual height was more likely to be around 21 inches, increasing to about 30 inches by the end of the century.

Dwarf candlesticks and chamber candlesticks in Sheffield plate were also produced in great numbers. The former, usually measuring five to seven inches in height, had numerous uses in the average home. The latter, complete with snuffer, was intended for carrying around the house and might be around three to four inches in height with a shallow base approximately six inches in diameter, generally following the styles of contemporary silver types. Snuffers were discontinued after about 1844. There was always the danger of a fire starting from such unprotected flames, and a later type of chamber candlestick, made in the first four decades or so of the nineteenth century, was designed with its candle socket protected by a glass shade. There was also a variation which incorporated a cylindrical glass chimney.

Sheffield plate chamber candlestick with replacement extinguisher, *circa* 1820. The mark inside the nozzle is N.

Also very popular in Sheffield plate was the tray which was made throughout the entire period of Sheffield plate. Prior to the 1760s when the plate was silvered on one side only, the tray was not uncommonly made of two sheets of plate, placed back to back and then soldered together, greatly contributing to its increased cost. Less expensive examples had the underside tinned. When the technique progressed so that the copper could be fused on both sides with silver, trays were generally produced in the new plate as well. Many late eighteenth century trays were made in an oval shape – with thread or beaded edges of sterling silver, perhaps bright-cut – and also in a rectangular shape with their ends formed attractively as handles, perhaps in a scroll outline. Some had beautiful pierced edges. Larger rectangular trays, variously decorated, appeared during the first few years of the nineteenth century.

An interesting branch of the Sheffield plate industry was that of wire-work. The method of plating wire dates from 1768 when fine strips of silver were wrapped around copper rods, and then fused to the copper in the usual way. The plated rod was then repeatedly put through an instrument pierced with holes, starting at about one inch in diameter and decreasing down to the required diameter of the wire. After constant annealing the plated rod finally emerged as plated wire. The technique was improved upon in the 1780s and, within about ten years, the manufacture of plated wire became a specialised section of the industry. It was used variously, but was of particular importance in the production of delightful fruit and cake baskets, sugar baskets, sugar vases and épergnes, whose method of manufacture was simple. The wire was cut to the correct lengths, inserted into holes in the rim and base, and secured by solder. Designs were numerous, again generally reflecting the styles set by silversmiths who had been producing baskets in sterling silver wire in increasing quantities since about 1760, their fashion gradually declining during the reign of George IV.

Button-making was an important industry in its own right. By the 1770s it is recorded that over 80 master button-makers, producing all types of buttons, were working in Birmingham where button-making had been prolific for over 100 years. Sheffield plate was ideal for this purpose and had been used for button-making since it was discovered by Thomas Boulsover *circa* 1742. By the 1780s Birmingham button-makers produced large quantities of buttons and included among their numbers Matthew Boulton's Button Company which was started in 1782. Sheffield plate had gained for itself such a good reputation as a substance for button-making that an Act was passed in 1796 which regulated the quality of metals used for buttons. This Act also stated that plated buttons were to be made from copper to which silver had been affixed by fusing, thus eliminating the use of silvered or other inferior covering being sold as Sheffield plate. An amazing variety of Sheffield plate buttons was produced, including hunting buttons with a central motif and the name of the hunt around the side, racing buttons, shooting buttons, cockfighting buttons, livery buttons and gilded buttons for the uniforms of officers. Early buttons were shaped by hand, but after the 1780s they were die-stamped. Mechanisation gradually speeded up and increased production and by the third decade of the nineteenth century the range had become so diverse that a manufacturer might have over a thousand pairs of dies for stamping arms, crests and motifs of various types.

There is a large selection of items from which to choose, therefore, for those with an interest in Sheffield plate, the list of domestic wares and personal objects such as snuff boxes being extensive and all-embracing. Apart from the more ubiquitous pieces there are also charming examples of bygone objects which have a curious fascination of their own. Such an item was the chafing ball. This was a highly desirable object in winter, intended to keep hands warm, perhaps tucked into pockets. With the price of heating fuel at its present level they may be due for a revival in a modern version! They were simply a decoratively-pierced hollow ball about four inches in diameter which opened to reveal a heater or spirit lamp of suitably diminutive measurements swinging in the centre of a gimbal which retained it in a safe position.

Before the invention of friction matches the pipelighter or charcoal brazier must have been of great assistance to the clay-pipe smoker. This was virtually a small pan for holding a smoker's continuous 'light' in the form of glowing charcoal, which generally stood upon a tripod or three short legs above the surface of the table, usually with an attractively-pierced rim. On an accompanying tray were placed small ember tongs, used to pick up the charcoal, with which the smoker would ignite his tobacco. There were probably other uses for this long-defunct object.

Sheffield plate snuff box, *circa* 1785, possibly made by Joseph Wilson, founder of the Sharrow Snuff Mills in Sheffield, and an associate of Thomas Boulsover for a time.

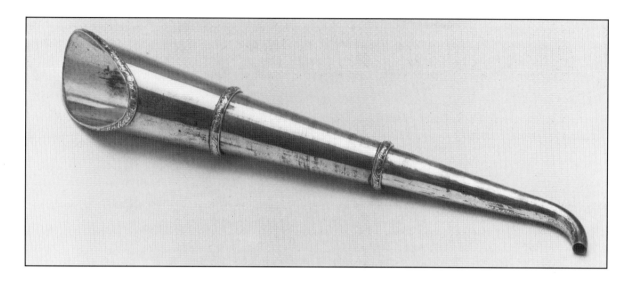

During a period when oysters were not regarded as the luxury they are today, attractive scallop-shells were produced in both Sheffield plate and sterling silver, complete with small cockle-shell feet, to contain oysters baked in a delicious sauce or cream with a scattering of crisply-browned breadcrumbs on the top. Such shells had other uses at the table, depending upon requirements, perhaps for butter or succulent fish dishes. They were generally sold in sets of four or six, varying a little in form over the years. They would still have a use today, unlike the practical hot-water plate, a useful device popular for many years, which was originally hand-made but later machine-stamped. The plates or pans consisted of two sections, upper and lower, the latter being fitted with a screw-cap filler into which the hot water was poured so that food on top would stay warm.

Sheffield plate telescopic ear trumpet, *circa* 1820, length approximately 12 inches.

While there was a wide miscellany of domestic objects in Sheffield plate pouring forth from Sheffield and Birmingham, it must not be forgotten that there were also large quantities of cheap, badly-plated wares being imported from France. To some extent these imports were responsible for English manufacturers constantly seeking means to produce a cheaper plate. Collectors should watch out for imported plate, generally spun and of a poor quality since it is greatly inferior. It is not too difficult to detect. Quite apart from the fact that it looks cheap and is light in weight, the colour is distinctive, having a reddish glow usually deeper than that of English plate where the silver is worn. In fact, since the copper is of a denser shade and the silver extremely thin it imparts a pink colouring in some cases to the actual plate.

6 | Electro-plate

Electro-plate produced during the nineteenth century may become as collectable as certain other pieces of Victoriana, and for the beginner in particular it has several other things to commend it. At the moment it is usually very reasonably priced. It is also interesting since it reflects the amazing conglomeration of styles which jockeyed with each other for a place of supremacy in Victorian fashion. Also, although the age of mass-production had established itself, some of the hand techniques used in the making of Sheffield plate or sterling silver wares were retained and used for some years on their electro-plated counterparts. The colour of early electro-plate, although not comparable with sterling silver or Sheffield plate, is also far more mellow than the harsh tones of modern electro-plate. Certain examples, particularly teapots and coffee pots, were quite robust considering their low cost then and now, and in some cases might even be described as sturdy compared with the lightweight objects produced today.

As in the case of Sheffield plate, the collecting potential is vast since so many objects were electro-plated. An additional advantage is that a great quantity of cutlery was electro-plated and today sets of a dozen pieces or so can be bought for a few pounds, providing time is taken to browse and choose with care. All in all, therefore, this much-maligned method of plating deserves a chapter in this book for, quite apart from the points mentioned, a potential collector intending to take the subject fairly seriously cannot help but acquire a knowledge of Victorian styles and decoration which will stand him in good stead when it comes to spending larger sums on sterling silver.

The young Queen Victoria had been on the throne for a short while when a patent was taken out by G. R. Elkington and O. W. Barratt which was to have far-reaching effects on the plating industry in England. It was concerned with a new process for coating metals with zinc in a revolutionary way which was far removed from the working of metal by fire, the method used since ancient times. By the wording in which the patent was couched it is thought that a single-cell battery was used, an idea which was not new to scientists who had been working on experiments in electro-metallurgy following Alessandro Volta's invention of an electric battery in 1800. Only five years later, in 1805, Brugnatelli made history by using electrolysis to coat two silver medals with gold. Although this was a big step forward there were still many technical problems to be resolved, among which were those of achieving an even deposit over the complete surface of the piece and also of getting this to adhere permanently.

ELECTRO AND SILVER PLATING

SKETCHED AT THE WORKS OF MESSRS. ELKINGTON AND CO., VISITED BY H.R.H. THE PRINCE OF WALES

MODELLING

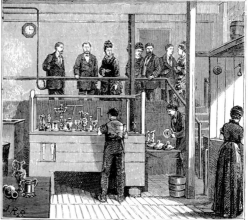

GOLD PLATING

SMALL STAMP

ENTRANCE TO THE WORKS

SOLDERING

STEAM STAMPING

ENAMELLING

Experimental work continued and much progress was made until by 1840 a doctor by the name of John Wright had hit upon the answer. He had been using solutions of cyanides of gold and silver in cyanide of potassium in his experiments, and had met with considerable success in solving the problem of a consistent adhesive coating of silver. In that year he entered into partnership with Elkington and Company, selling them the secrets of his discovery for a sum of money and royalties on all silver deposited on electro-plate as well as all licences granted under the patent. It would appear that his business acumen matched his scientific ability.

Before the idea could become a viable commercial proposition, however, more work needed to be carried out and during the years which followed Elkingtons applied for revised patents. One such is of great interest and importance since it concerned the making of electrotypes of existing pieces of silver, by causing either silver or gold to be deposited by electrical means in or on suitable models. A few years later another Elkington patent dealt with a new technique for producing a gold design on silver or other metal surfaces. The method was simple but effective and in its final stages allowed the gold design to be made permanent by the electric process of gilding. By the concluding years of the 1840s further developments made possible the inclusion of sulphur or carbon compounds to the solutions of metal which gave the object a more lustrous surface during the electro-deposition. In only a few years since John Wright had made his discovery, electro-plating was thus well on the way to becoming an established process. Elkingtons had shrewdly purchased the patents for electro-plating methods which had been taken out by others at that time, in order that competition would be eliminated as far as possible, so the commercial potential was enormous. Future years were to prove just how vast.

One of the reasons for the difference in colour between old Sheffield plate and electro-plate is the quality of the silver which was used. The former, as has already been stated, used silver of sterling quality (925 fine). Electro-plated wares and objects required pure silver. This accounts for the brighter, harsher colour of electro-plate and can help collectors to tell at a glance whether a piece is made of old Sheffield plate or electro-plate, although the latter also mellows with age. The detail of the ornament on electro-plate, depending on which type, may also be rather 'masked'. To differentiate between the two techniques it was not uncommon for manufacturers of Sheffield plate or British plate made after the introduction of electro-plate to describe their products as 'plated by fire', a term which implied superiority over electro-deposition, during which process minute particles of silver were taken from a sheet of pure silver – hung in the vat – by an electric current and deposited onto the surface of the base metal. On its removal burnishing, a task allotted to women, was necessary.

Before the objects were placed in the vat they were generally made by the usual methods of silversmithing. Some of the earlier items were first cast in German silver or Britannia metal. Progress in stamping later hastened and cheapened production. When the vessel had been hammered up from the flat, spun or cast, its ancillary parts previously

Far left: electro-plating works of Elkington and Company.

stamped out and joined by solder, it was ready for decorating. This might be achieved by the ancient method of hand-engraving, by the mechanical means of a lathe such as engine-turning, or by the technique of etching which emulated hand-engraving. Other types of decoration included piercing, usually punched automatically, speedily and cheaply. When all decoration was completed the object would be placed in the plating vat for electro-deposition.

Above left: burnishing electro-plated objects – a job usually reserved for women.

Above right: electro-plating vats.

Elkingtons entered into various business agreements, one of which was with Benjamin Smith to whose London firm they agreed to supply plated goods which would be stamped with Smith's mark. Benjamin Smith's son married G. R. Elkington's daughter, so financial arrangements were still kept very much within the family. Later it was agreed that Smith should be allowed to manufacture as well as to sell electro-plated goods in London. Affairs did not work out quite as planned, however, and in 1848 G. R. Elkington bought up Smith's interests including the Regent Street and Moorgate premises, conducting his own business at the former. The Birmingham branch continued under the name of Elkington, Mason and Company. While Elkingtons were carrying out experiments and taking out patents for new processes during the 1840s, various firms were producing electro-plated goods under licence to Elkingtons, although originally Elkingtons had hoped to get these firms to send the manufactured objects to Birmingham for the actual plating. However, the idea was not practical since it was hardly economically sound for firms to do this.

As early as 1842 it was agreed that Barnards of London should have a licence to electro-plate their own products, under the supervision of an Elkington employee, for an agreed payment and a percentage on all goods plated for a certain period of time. This set a precedent for similar licences which were issued during the next few years, and because of this and other factors, the commercial viability of electro-plating made

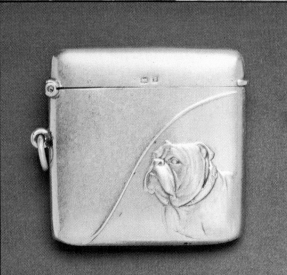

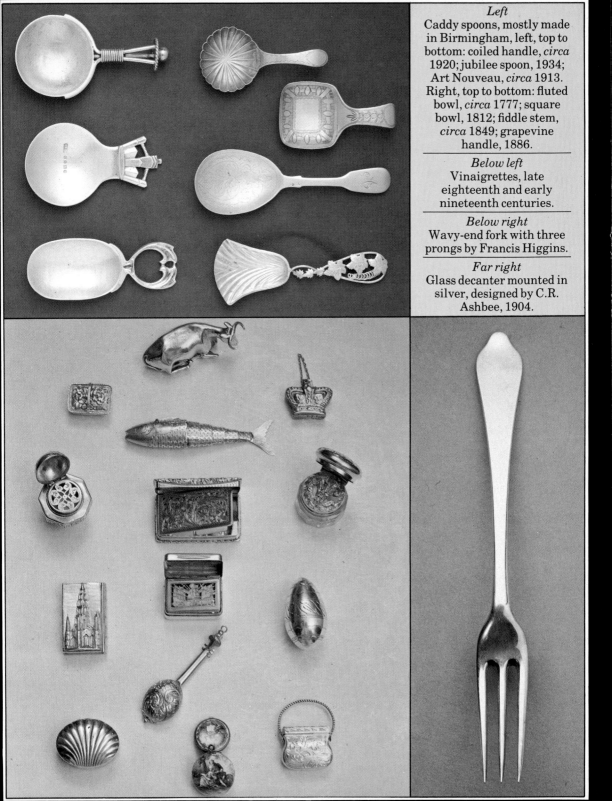

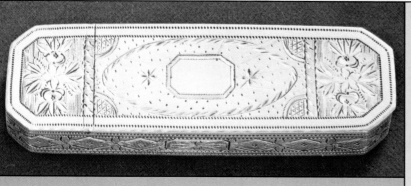

Left
Toothpick case by Samuel Pemberton, Birmingham, 1791.

Below left
Cup and cover in sterling silver, set with five opals, made in Birmingham, 1902, for Liberty and Company.

Below right
Silver shaving brush made in London, *circa* 1797.

in-roads into the plating industry, and soon superseded Sheffield plate. After four or five years licences were issued to numerous firms in London, Birmingham and Sheffield, and the terms became less stringent as the time limit of the Elkington patent lessened.

Electro-plating was so firmly established by the time of the Great Exhibition in 1851 that several firms featured a prominent display of the new electro-plated goods. Among those who continued to produce Sheffield plate were Bradbury's and James Dixon and Sons, the latter also showing electro-plated items. Apart from the immediate commercial effects of electro-plating, the long-term connotations enabled Elkingtons to encourage and promote the work of artists and designers such as Albert Wilms and L. Morel Ladeuil. Other manufacturers, too, were able to encourage such designers, producing pieces in silver and electro-plate under the banner of Felix Summerly's Art Manufacturers, an organisation of artists, designers and manufacturers set up by the eminent designer Henry Cole in 1847 to produce new works and, in the organisation's own words, 'to revive the good old practice of connecting the best art with familiar objects in everyday use'. Manufacturers who were connected with the organisation and who made their pieces included James Dixon and Sons, Broadhead and Atkin, Joseph Rodgers and Sons and Benjamin Smith.

Among the artists and designers who produced work for Felix Summerly's Art Manufacturers were Richard Redgrave, whose designs included a set of knives adorned with ornament representing fish, flesh, fowl and game; John Bell, whose cutlery included dessert knives and forks embellished with fruit, and fish knives and forks decorated with fish and boys fishing; J. C. Horsley, whose decanter stoppers included vintagers, gathering the grapes, wine-making and wine made and, since Horsley also designed the first Christmas card depicting a convivial scene of people drinking, small wonder that the prudish and hypocritical outlook of certain Victorians was reflected in their comments that the card encouraged alcoholic imbibing. Other electro-plated wares produced by this select group of creative artists and designers included a teapot designed by Redgrave which was a fantastic creation called Camellia,

Electro-plated items, left to right: hot-water jug, *circa* 1865; biscuit box with rustic frame; side view of a similar biscuit box, *circa* 1880-1900; cylindrical jug, *circa* 1870; coffee pot by James Dixon and Sons.

topped by a Chinese fairy examining a tea-plant made in Parian porcelain by Mintons; a tea-caddy spoon, designed by Harry Rodgers, and decorated with the ever-popular tea-plant; and a salt cellar, designed by H. J. Townsend called the Infant Neptune.

Naturalism played as important a role in the ornament on electro-plated wares as it did on sterling silver, the electrotype providing invaluable assistance to modellers. Natural items such as ferns and flowers as well as small creatures such as lizards were sometimes preserved in a metal coating so that the designer and modeller could convey their forms onto plate by precise observation of the real thing, for perfection in naturalism was something for which designers strove. Electrotypes were not confined to natural items, however. There is an electrotype of the Mostyn salt of 1581 in the Victoria and Albert Museum, London, which bears the original Elizabethan hallmarks since the Assay Office failed to notice and obliterate them. Electrotypes were also made of both Japanese metalwork when Japanese styles became fashionable from the late 1870s, and of contemporary works including a vase made by Hunt and Roskell presented as a wedding gift to the Prince and Princess of Wales.

The famous Hunt and Roskell firm was descended from the firm of Storr and Mortimer of which the eminent Regency silversmith Paul Storr became a partner in 1822. Some 14 years later Paul Storr's nephew, John Samuel Hunt, became a third partner and when Storr retired in 1838 the firm became known as Mortimer and Hunt. Upon the retirement of Mortimer, Robert Roskell became a partner and the firm changed its name again to Hunt and Roskell. During the Great Exhibition of 1851 Hunt and Roskell exhibited, among other impressive naturalistic pieces of plate, two candelabra with their stems and branches consisting of a vine on a base of Indian architecture, dessert stands of flowering naturalistic form with Indian figures and ice-pails inspired by the lotus and enlivened with Indian plants. These pieces were part of a service made as a testimonial to the Earl of Ellenborough in recognition of his work in India and, although not within the reach of the ordinary man, were the sort of examples which were important since they influenced the design of future silver and plated goods in general.

The designs which Christopher Dresser produced for electro-plated wares were in direct contrast to contemporary ideas on style. Reactionary in their simplicity and functionalism, their clear, uncluttered outlines stand out from the styles already described in chapter 3. The Victoria and Albert Museum, London, has an electro-plated Dresser tea set which he designed for James Dixon and Sons. Today there is nothing extraordinary about it but how it must have amazed people then. It is based on a spherical shape devoid of decoration. The sugar bowl, milk jug and teapot all stand upon three simple feet, the latter two having neat functional handles which break away completely from the scroll form or anything derived from this outline, emphasising instead a vertical grip which follows the spherical shapes of the vessels. The set is beautifully designed even by modern standards and could quite easily have been produced within recent years. In fact it bears the Registry mark for 1880, when our forefathers were enamoured with everything opposed to it in design and ornament.

It also says much for James Dixon and Sons that they were prepared to sponsor such progressive ideas, as were Hukin and Heath who produced a wide miscellany of domestic electro-plated articles and secured the services of Christopher Dresser to advise them on design. Under his guidance they produced some beautifully simple and well-proportioned objects for everyday use in the home. The interesting point about Christopher Dresser was that, while he had very definite and original ideas on design, he never veered from his intention of being a commercial designer. He produced designs for Elkingtons, too. He once wrote that 'if the designer forms works which are expensive, he places them beyond the reach of those who might otherwise enjoy them'. His designs for electro-plated wares certainly did not fall into such a category.

While items by eminent designers may be out of the price range of many collectors, it is possible to hunt around and discover examples which show their influence, or to specialise in collecting pieces after a certain style. Such styles (see chapter 3) might include Japanese-inspired pieces, the vogue for which was intense throughout the domestic scene and elsewhere and for which, among others, Christopher Dresser in the late 1870s opened an Oriental warehouse in Farringdon Road 'for the exhibition and sale of decorative objects of all kinds imported from Japan, China and India'; Adam or Louis Seize wares, very popular during the 1880s and echoing in some ways the neo-classical period of the late eighteenth century, incorporating acanthus leaves, swags and bows with much engraving and centre shields, particularly on teapots and larger pieces of domestic wares; a revived rococo, very much apparent during the last two decades; and pieces showing certain Huguenot-style forms of decoration of the early eighteenth century, emulated with much enthusiasm.

The most important influence at this time was, of course, that of Art Nouveau, with its easy flowing lines of grace and elegance which found favour with, among others, the comparatively new firm of Liberty and

Above left: electro-plated double dish designed by Christopher Dresser and made by Hukin and Heath, *circa* 1880.

Above right: Victorian biscuit box in the Japanese style, by Elkington and Company, 1881.

Company. Art Nouveau, with its sinuous lines emulating the lotus or the lily, is hard to define since its inspiration in general was derived from an unlikely combination of Japanese and mediæval ideas. It proved eminently adaptable to practically all vessel shapes and numerous other types of domestic objects. In a more modified form it influenced electro-plate nearly as much as sterling silver and can still sometimes be seen in the lines of pieces produced as late as the early 1920s. I noted just such a piece prior to the time of writing in the form of an Art Nouveau electro-plated cigarette box in a shop some 30 miles from London. It was an excellent buy at under £10. A set of electro-plated fish knives and forks was also seen at the same time bearing a series of impressive marks which a cursory glance might take to be sterling silver hallmarks, which might have fooled the unwary (see chapter 4).

Electro-plated bachelor's three-piece tea set and fan-shaped tray, *en suite*, engraved with bamboos, birds and butterflies, *circa* 1880.

Collectors of nineteenth century plated objects should be aware of a registry mark which was sometimes stamped upon miscellaneous items between 1842 and 1883 inclusive. The mark proves that the piece was registered at the British Patent Office, and from it the date of registration can be deduced as well as a guide to the name of the patentee. Items were divided into classes and those of Sheffield plate or electro-plate came into Class I. The mark takes the shape of a lozenge, above the top apex of which (facing) is a small circle in which is inscribed the class of the goods. Inside the lozenge beneath the circle appears the year letter. The left angle of the lozenge contains the month and the right angle the day. The number for the bundle or parcel of goods appears in the bottom angle. The year letters for 1842 to 1867 are as follows: 1842 X; 1843 H; 1844 C; 1845 A; 1846 I; 1847 F; 1848 U; 1849 S; 1850 V; 1851 P; 1852 D; 1853 Y; 1854 J; 1855 E; 1856 L; 1857 K; 1858 B; 1859 M; 1860 Z; 1861 R; 1862 O; 1863 G; 1864 N; 1865 W; 1866 Q; and 1867 T. Month letters: January C; February G; March W; April H; May E; June M; July I; August R; September D; October B; November K; and December·A.

From 1868 to 1883, although the lozenge remained the same, the information was put in a different angle within it. The class remained in the circle above the top apex. The day appeared beneath this, the number of the bundle or parcel of goods in the angle to the left and the year in the angle to the right, with the month appearing in the angle at the bottom. Year letters for 1868 to 1883 were: 1868 X; 1869 H; 1870 C; 1871 A; 1872 I; 1873 F; 1874 U; 1875 S; 1876 V; 1877 P; 1878 D; 1879 Y; 1880 J; 1881 E; 1882 L; and 1883 K. Month letters: January C; February G; March W; April H; May E; June M; July I; August R; September D; October B; November K; and December A. From 1 to 6 March 1878 the letters G and W were used for month and year respectively. After the year 1883 the lozenge was abandoned and a serial number replaced it which was used for all types of objects. The following are from 1884 to 1895: 1884 – I; 1885 – 19754; 1886 – 40480; 1887 – 64520; 1888 – 90483; 1889 – 116648; 1890 – 141273; 1891 – 163767; 1892 – 185713; 1893 – 205240; 1894 – 224720; and 1895 – 246975.

7 | Caring for Silver

The lustre and mellow colour, characteristic of old silver, which distinguish it from the colder, metallic appearance of new wares, will be enhanced by regular, careful cleaning and polishing. A circular movement, not a backward-and-forward one, should always be adopted when cleaning or drying silver to prevent abrasion. It should also be noted that larger pieces of silver should not be cleaned on a hard surface such as a table-top, but should be held against the body so that hard pressure is not exerted on the piece.

Silver should be cleaned regularly to prevent damage by heavy tarnish. Never use any method of cleaning which involves undue friction or abrasion; always use a cleaner intended specifically for the purpose. Tarnishing results from the reaction of the silver with various compounds of sulphur which are present in the air and certain foods. Such compounds combine with the silver on its surface to form a film of silver sulphide, and it is this which causes the silver to discolour. The most important sources of tarnish-forming sulphur compounds include gases from the burning of oil, coal gas, logs, coal or petrol; and foodstuffs such as eggs, fish, peas, vinegar and lemon juice.

One of the worst enemies of silver is salt, which corrodes all silverware. Because of this, salt cellars should be emptied immediately after use and washed at once, together with any items such as salt spoons which may have come into contact with the salt. Glass liners do not necessarily prevent corrosion since the salt often slips between the liner and the silver casing. Salt will not affect a gilt-lined cellar, providing the gilt is not worn. If this is the case, the salt can reach the silver beneath and corrosion will therefore occur.

New products have been introduced over recent years for the cleaning and polishing of silver. Certain good-quality polishes are safe to use on most silver providing the instructions are strictly observed. If in any doubt write to the firm which makes the cleaner: their technical staff will be happy in most cases to give you guidance. Some polishes have definite advantages, including the saving of time and the lessening of abrasion. Among the various types of cleaners available, Goddard's produce a polish which also contains a long term ingredient that forms an invisible, chemical barrier on the surface of the silver, thus inhibiting tarnish so silver remains cleaner for a longer period. Also available is a long term silver foam which penetrates the crevices and grooves in more intricate and elaborate decorative work. The foam is then rinsed off and the silver is ready to be dried thoroughly with a soft cloth. No water should ever be left on silver, since most water contains chlorine which will discolour it. After washing, dry thoroughly, particularly the more ornate pieces.

For silver cutlery there is a cleaner in the form of a liquid silver dip in which the pieces are placed for a few minutes to remove any tarnish, and afterwards carefully rinsed then dried and polished. This can be done with a special long term silver cloth which is particularly useful for polishing ornaments which are kept permanently on display and which need frequent attention to keep them in excellent condition. They will only need a short, light rubbing action if polished regularly.

An intermediate wash will do your silver no harm. Wash the silver in warm or hot soapy water or, perhaps, a mild detergent. Rinse it thoroughly and dry it with a soft cloth or chamois leather. Silver-gilt also should be cleaned carefully with warm soapy water, then rinsed and gently dried on a soft cloth. Never use a brush or anything harsh which could damage the surface of the piece. Expert advice should always be sought on more complicated problems such as the removal of black spot, verdigris and lacquer from silver and silver-gilt.

Silver and silver-gilt should be stored in tissue paper since this generally contains very little sulphur; in fact, specially-treated sulphur-free paper may be bought from most good jewellers. Never store silver in newspaper, brown paper or blankets. Rubber bands should not be used when storing silver, as rubber is particularly rich in sulphur.

It is vital that all silver should be realistically insured. Certain dealers will value silver and usually charge a percentage of the value of the piece as their fee. You should draw the attention of your insurance company to the fact that objects are antiques when this is so, since they will therefore appreciate in value. The insurance company can then give you an estimate for a premium which will provide the correct kind of coverage. Objects which exceed certain amounts will usually need to be mentioned as individual pieces. It is always a good idea to take photographs of any items which you particularly prize since, in the event of a burglary, these can sometimes be of assistance to the police in the recovery of valuables.

Two early advertisements for Goddard's Plate Powder.

Part 2 COLLECTING SILVER

8 | Flatware

In the twentieth century it is difficult to imagine eating meals without the aid of cutlery, yet it was not until the eighteenth century that it became the general custom to use forks, knives and spoons. The habit spread only gradually. Towards the later years of the seventeenth century a host might be expected to provide cutlery at table and although this tendency increased, many travellers carried with them their own personal set of a fork, knife and spoon, in a case often made of tooled leather, until as late as around the middle of the eighteenth century.

Miscellaneous items including, top, sugar nippers; top, left to right: cheese scoop, ladles and marrow scoop; second row, left to right: fork, sugar sifter spoon, tea spoon, spoon with decorative bowl (at back); centre: ladle; third row: wine labels. All eighteenth or early nineteenth century.

Spoons

Spoons made their appearance far earlier than forks and knives. The history of the silver spoon is a long and ancient one and the craft of the spooner can be traced back at least to the Middle Ages. Earlier spoons are rare and hardly any specimens remain to show us how the spoon developed after the Romans left these shores. As far as silver spoons are concerned, it was not until considerably later, during the thirteenth century, that these began to be used for domestic purposes, and then only by the court and nobles of the land. Neither did they look much like the elegant utensils to which we are accustomed. Crude and functional until around the middle of the seventeenth century, they were hammered into shape from a single piece of silver, their only concession to decoration being in the ornamental knop, which was sometimes gilt, cast and then soldered into a notch at the stem terminal. The bowls were shaped for the specific purpose of lifting food into the mouth and were not suitable for liquids until later when they became deeper. Very early stems were diamond-shaped, followed by a hexagonal form, both of which tapered slightly towards the knop.

Knops are of great interest since they took various decorative forms. They included a simple diamond-shaped point; an acorn; a moor's head; a wrythen (a ball marked with spiral twistings); a woodwose (wildman with a club); a ball; a lion sejant; and seal tops. Worthy of special mention is the maidenhead knop, a popular sixteenth century shape, although in fact one of the earliest types since it is noted in a will long before the sixteenth century. Silver spoons, it must be remembered, were greatly-cherished personal items which were bequeathed to loved ones with other precious belongings. The Virgin Mary inspired the maidenhead knop, the head-dress of which was particularly interesting since it tended to reflect current styles of fashion, changing as these did over the years.

Apostle spoons are well-known among spoons with decorative knops. They were available singly or in sets of 13, the thirteenth spoon bearing a figure of Christ in Majesty. It was customary to give an apostle spoon as a christening present, the child receiving the spoon depicting the saint after whom he was named, although this custom began to wane after the middle years of the seventeenth century. The apostles included: St Peter who carried a key, two keys or a fish; St John with a chalice, eagle or palm branch; St Andrew carrying a saltire cross; St James the Greater with a staff or other pilgrim appendages; St James the Less with a fuller's bat because he was killed by a blow on the head from Simeon the fuller; St Philip bearing a pastoral staff and sometimes a basket of bread; St Bartholomew with a butcher's knife; St Simon Zelotes, a long saw; St Thomas, a spear; St Jude, a cross or club; St Matthias, an axe or lance; St Matthew, a wallet and sometimes an axe; and St Paul with a sword. Such spoons command exceedingly high prices. They have been copied throughout the centuries and even today modern reproductions are made. Quite apart from these genuine reproductions, which can in themselves be deceptive since with a little age they can resemble very easily their originals, there are also faked examples in circulation.

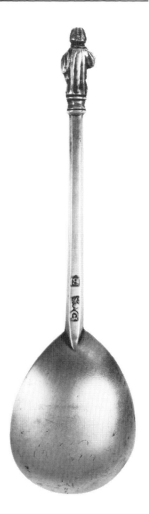

Elizabethan apostle spoon, London, 1599, showing the maker's mark at the lower end of the stem.

During the seventeenth century further changes evolved in the shape of the spoon, including the slipped-in-the-stalk spoon which had begun to appear earlier, still being made from a single piece of silver, with perhaps the owner's initials pricked upon the slanting termination of the stem or sometimes in the bowl. The Puritan spoon had developed by about 1650, and began to resemble spoons as we know them today. The end of its stem was cut off squarely and inconspicuously, and was devoid of a knop. The broad, flat stem joined the near-elliptical bowl at the back with a small V-shape. Following the Restoration in 1660 the square Puritan end gave way to the trifid-end spoon which simply meant that the square shape was hammered out into a thin, rounded leaf form which was divided by two deep notches or cuts near to each side, making three sections and forming a simple trefoil. Originally the sections or lobes were unequal, the outer two being smaller, but later examples had equal sections. The oval bowl and stem were strengthened at the back by a tapering rib which strengthened the junction of stem and bowl, the forerunner of the rat-tail which became general shortly after this.

A pair of decorated trifid spoons by Lawrence Coles, London, 1705.

Later the backs of the bowls around the rat-tail were decorated with scroll-work in low relief, as might be the upper side of the end of the stem. Others were quite plain, or might be engraved with a crest or sometimes initials. The usual size was around six-and-a-half inches in length, although larger examples were also made which measured up to about eight inches. Towards the end of the seventeenth century the pronounced trifid shape lessened, and the cuts or notches at the end of the stem disappeared and developed into a central curve with a lesser one resembling a curved shoulder on either side. This is known as the wavy-end spoon. Sometimes the rat-tail at the back of the bowl might be decorated with small beading. Both trifid and wavy-end spoons have much primitive charm and, although costly, are among the rarer spoons to which collectors can eventually aspire. They can do this by building up a collection of less costly sterling silver spoons and trading them in at a later date. Good examples of the above-mentioned spoons can be seen at the Victoria and Albert Museum, London.

A few years after the turn of the eighteenth century the spoon eventually developed into the utensil which we use today. By 1720 its stem had become gracefully curved and terminated in a flat, rounded end which turned forward or upward and upon which it was rested on the table, so that the back of the bowl was uppermost in the French way. This Hanoverian rat-tail spoon continued in fashion for a few more years, the rat-tail gradually disappearing to be replaced by small droplets, either one or two, at the back of the bowl, or the increasingly fashionable scallop-shell, typical of the rococo period. The stem evolved into a flatter form, terminating by the 1760s in a curve which turned in the opposite direction to its predecessor, ie backward instead of forward, so that the spoon could be placed on the table with the interior of its bowl showing, as is still the custom in England and elsewhere today. This is termed the 'Old English' pattern and has been the basic form for spoons ever since.

A variety of decoration began to adorn this shape. Over successive years ornament included the very popular and attractive feather-edge engraving comprising a border engraved with short, feathery slanting lines; bright-cutting, the delightful faceted type of engraving; and the simple threaded edge. The Onslow pattern, named after Arthur Onslow (1691-1768) who was Speaker of the House of Commons for 33 years, was an earlier design, appearing before the middle of the eighteenth century. Its stem terminated in an unusual curled and reeded volute which tapered gracefully into the stem, thus successfully combining the ornate with the elegant.

Within about 20 years of the turn of the eighteenth century spoons of different sizes became more usual and the table spoon as distinct from the dessert spoon emerged. Tea spoons were produced in growing numbers as the British addiction to tea intensified, despite the horrifyingly high cost of the beverage. The fiddle pattern had appeared by the end of the eighteenth century, growing in popularity during the following century, and still remaining popular today. The fiddle stem comprised square shoulders above the bowl junction. The stem end was rounded with inward-directed shoulders graduating into the shaft of the stem. The fiddle pattern might be either plain or decorated with contemporary ornament. Also making their appearance at this time were the ornate King's pattern and similarly opulent Queen's pattern, both based on the fiddle pattern and incorporating anthemion and shells in relief at their decorative stem terminals, with scrolled and threaded edges. These, too, remain fashionable today. Such designs appeared on flatware generally.

Above: ladle with Onslow design stem terminal, London, 1796.

Left: flatware, fiddle shape, with decorative Queen's pattern, London, *circa* 1878, and London and Dublin, 1835-1953.

Flatware, fiddle shape, decorated with thread and shell, George Angell, London, 1846.

Fancy-back or picture-back spoons mostly date from about 1740 but are more numerous after about 1760, though earlier examples are known. Most picture-back spoons are tea spoons, although other sizes were made, but picture-back dessert spoons are rare. Picture-back tea spoons are exceedingly varied and attractive. They were produced by various spoon-makers, perhaps die-struck or with cast ornament, and their pictures or patterns were often similar, but it is unknown whether this is because early examples were copied from a pattern book or whether the makers simply copied each other. Some designs were politically motivated, such as the dove holding an olive branch – also found on American spoons – which was in all probability inspired by the abortive Olive Branch petition from the American Colonists to George III in 1775, although the King refused to meet Richard Penn. Other designs and pictures included shell and scroll backs; a delightful pyriform teapot; sprays of flowers; a vase of flowers; a hen with chicks in a farmyard scene; swans; a milkmaid with pails; and various animals. Picture-back spoons, although scarce, are not impossible to find, particularly in remote markets or shops where they fetch sums far below their usual cost. Important eighteenth century spoon-makers include Thomas Chawner, Daniel Smith and Robert Sharp; George Heming and William Chawner; John Wakelin and William Taylor; and John Crouch and Thomas Hannam.

Most specific-purpose spoons appeared later in the eighteenth century. *Mustard spoons* were introduced during about the third quarter of the eighteenth century and, while the decoration on the stem was the same as other flatware at that time, the bowl was distinctive because of its unusual fig shape, a form which was also followed by early *egg spoons*. These generally began to filter into homes from the turn of the nineteenth century, though some examples, particularly those with silver-gilt bowls, date from the final years of the eighteenth century. They were generally sold as part of the fittings on egg frames. *Coffee spoons* were very late arrivals although they are recorded as early as the first few years of the eighteenth century in a vague context. Since tea spoons were small they no doubt doubled up for both purposes, and until the later years of the nineteenth century spoons made specifically for coffee were unusual. The old habit of taking salt on the blade of a knife was replaced with the introduction of *salt spoons*, which appeared as early as the first few years of the eighteenth century, their use increasing as did that of the salt cellar. Their bowls were commonly of a shovel shape, until the usual rounded form emerged towards the middle of the century. *Berry spoons*, used for fruit, appeared generally during the nineteenth century and later. Gilded, with heavy embossing of grapes and vine leaves or other naturalistic forms, they have been copied many times during this century. *Sugar sifter spoons*, with pierced ladle-shaped bowls, were used throughout the eighteenth century for the spreading of sugar on desserts or fruit at mealtimes. Very early examples date from about 1700.

Medicine spoons, however outdated they may seem today, played a vital role in the eighteenth and nineteenth centuries, enjoying popularity particularly in the latter period when the loathsome dose of castor-oil was administered. Medicine spoons took various forms, the most important two of which included a covered bowl and a double-bowl variety. The latter was usually about seven-and-a-half inches long with a small bowl at one end and a larger one at the other, used no doubt simply for varying quantities, or, as one theory has it, the smaller bowl possibly being for powdered forms of medicine. This type of spoon appeared from about the 1760s and various examples were produced.

The castor-oil spoon came into use during approximately the second decade or so of the nineteenth century. It consisted of a bowl with a cover which had an opening at one end and a circular, hollow handle or stem. The castor-oil was poured in, a finger held over the opening and the medicine was tipped quickly through the hole in the covered bowl into the mouth of the unfortunate victim. So successful was the idea that this type of spoon was still in use until at least the middle of the nineteenth century.

Other types of medicine spoons included an invalid's covered feeding spoon, similar to the castor-oil spoon but without the hollow handle, also in use during the nineteenth century, and a short-stemmed, single-bowl spoon which was generally used for measuring liquids and which appeared approximately during the middle of the eighteenth century.

Knives and forks

A knife and fork may seem the perfect combination by modern standards, but before forks came into general use the knife and the spoon were the two vital, complementary utensils which served the needs at table (see chapter 2). While eighteenth century examples of knives with handles of cast silver are available at a very high cost, the expense involved in making these in the heavier-gauge silver means that most eighteenth century examples available today are of the thinner silver produced at the end of the century.

Forks were used increasingly in England after the Restoration. The Victoria and Albert Museum, London, has a two-pronged fork made in 1632, one of the oldest silver table forks, but this is a very rare example. Later examples were three-pronged, usually followed by the four-pronged variety which we use today, although both types might also be made concurrently. Early fork handles resembled those of contemporary spoons and, as the use of forks increased during the eighteenth century, so the ornament and shapes described for spoon stems were reflected in fork designs. Apart from silver handles, forks might also be given handles of other materials including ivory, amber, mother-of-pearl and tortoiseshell, wood or bone.

Spoons and three-pronged forks, early eighteenth century.

Matching sets of cutlery were not very apparent until the later years of the seventeenth century and it was not until the eighteenth century that their use became more general. The dawn of the Georgian era saw the gradual appearance of matching knives and forks with cast silver hafts. Silver-handled knives and forks made during the final years of the eighteenth century may not be hallmarked, since those weighing under five pennyweights of silver were exempt after 1790. Instead, certain manufacturers applied the word Sterling, together with their own mark, and since by this time the cutlery industry of Sheffield had reached unprecedented sales, most cutlery so struck is likely to have come from that area.

Miscellaneous

A reminder of a custom long past in England is the *marrow scoop*, a utensil which was used exactly as its name implies: for scooping out the marrow from cooked marrow bones, a nutritional habit now extinct. Marrow scoops are numerous. They consist of a scoop at one end, shaped like an elongated spoon bowl, usually with a thinner type of scoop at the other end for penetrating narrow regions of the bone. Certain spoons have a marrow scoop at the end of their stems, and these are generally called marrow spoons, early examples of which are very rare. Usually hallmarks were punched on the reverse-side of the stem. Unlike the marrow scoop, *cheese scoops* can still fulfil a useful role at the table today. Late eighteenth century and nineteenth century examples are fairly common, consisting of a handle perhaps of wood, bone or mother-of-pearl into which has been inserted the tang of the shallow scoop for gouging out the cheese.

The *fish slice*, too, still has a practical use. Most eighteenth century examples dating from the last three decades of the century were attractively pierced with neo-classical or marine patterns, through which the fish juices were strained. Various decorative patterns in piercings followed during the nineteenth century. When handles were of silver their patterns generally matched those of the cutlery of the period. *Fish knives* were a far later idea and did not begin to filter into general usage until around the time after George IV had ascended the throne. *Asparagus servers* were earlier, appearing more generally during the last 30 years or so of the eighteenth century and usually shaped similarly to sugar tongs but larger, of course, and sometimes with a guiding spring between the two arms.

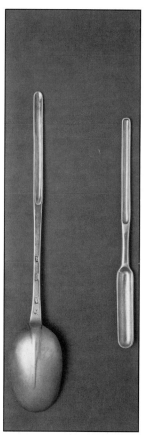

Above: left, marrow scoop and spoon, *circa* 1720; right, marrow scoop, *circa* 1738.

Left: close-up of pierced fish slice, *circa* 1810.

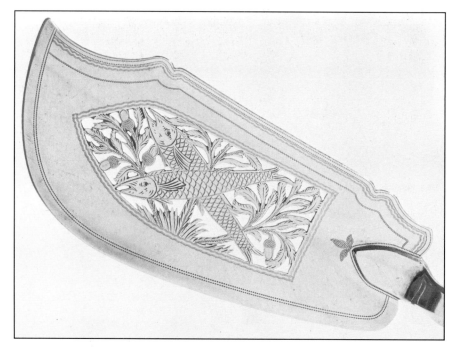

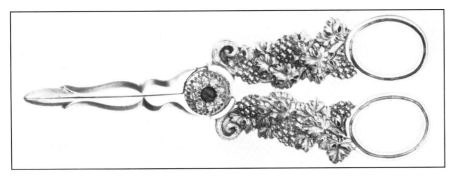

Top: King's pattern asparagus servers by Mary Chawner, London, 1836.

Left: grape shears by Charles Rawlings, 1825.

Grape scissors also date from the late eighteenth century, but such examples are rare. Mostly they were made from *circa* 1800. Early examples are simple and plain with ring handles and blades rather like sewing scissors. Later they were adorned with appropriate decoration in the form of grapes and vine foliage, and with one blade interlocking the other like garden secateurs. *Ladles* for soup and sauces were used from about 1760, their stems similar to contemporary flatware. *Pudding or pastry slices* also date from about this time, resembling fish slices, with ornament typical of each period.

Below: ladle of fine quality, *circa* 1740.

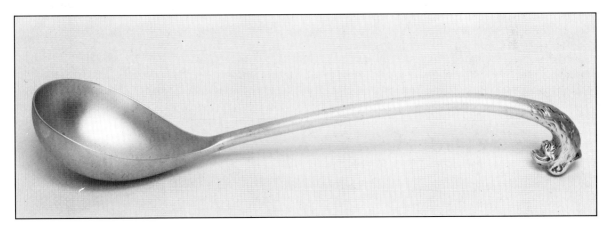

9 Tea Silver

Tea silver has always been among the most beautiful of domestic silver, and it has the added attraction that most of it is as practical today as it was when it was first made. Because of this it appeals particularly to those who like to use what they collect. When tea was first imported into England, only the wealthy could afford to drink it. They followed the influence of the court and since Charles II's queen, Catherine of Braganza, particularly enjoyed the beverage, drinking vast quantities of it in the solitude of her private rooms, it was not long before it was being drunk in the great houses throughout the land. It might cost as much as 50 shillings (£2·50) a pound and, although cheaper types were available, it was still too expensive and novel to take the place of the usual drinks such as ale or cider. However, the distinctive flavour of tea became increasingly popular and, by the time Queen Anne ascended the throne early in the eighteenth century, its future was assured.

Teapots

Comparatively few teapots were made in England before the eighteenth century and these are now exceedingly rare. As the fashion for drinking tea spread, the demand for the right kind of vessel in which to brew it brought about new types of containers for sugar, milk and tea. These tea accoutrements were made increasingly throughout the eighteenth century until, by the final decades, they had become an important branch of the silversmith's work. Late seventeenth century teapots are unique and are mostly seen in museums. Outstanding among them is the historical conical-topped teapot (1670) in the Victoria and Albert Museum, London, with the spout quaintly set at right-angles to the handle, a practice which was short-lived. Another shape of this early period looks like a melon or similar fruit.

Small, simple teapots shaped like plump pears, either completely circular or polygonal, were fashionable by the eighteenth century. Lids were generally hinged and swan-necked spouts were also often given a hinged flap at their opening, presumably to prevent heat loss. These little teapots, usually with wooden handles and perhaps a wooden finial upon their lids to prevent fingers from burning on the hot metal, remained popular for many years. They might be undecorated, chased, engraved or adorned with cut-card work. Certain examples were equipped with a stand beneath which was placed a spirit lamp.

From about 1720 another type appeared: the globular or bullet-shaped pot, with the spout opposite the handle which was by now the general

Above left: teapot with stand and lamp by Simon Pantin, London, 1705.

Above right: bullet teapot, London, 1720.

custom. In Scotland spherical teapots, standing upon a high stemmed foot, reached a perfection of shape which London silversmiths never quite produced, perhaps because the form was not so popular, or because they did not wish to emulate the Scottish craftsmen. By the 1730s the highly-decorative rococo influence became apparent on pieces of domestic silver, including teapots, and the simple vessel was embellished with scrolls and flowers, beautifully chased, its spout sometimes shaped like a dragon and the simple finial of previous decades replaced perhaps by the popular pineapple or a Chinaman. The Chinaman was typical of another decorative style at this time – the Orientally-inspired chinoiseries, the rococo version of which was pronounced and vigorous. Plain teapots were also produced. By the middle of the eighteenth century the somewhat ungainly inverted-pear shape emerged, with a short stem and wide foot-rim. Decoration generally included flat-chased borders or embossed rococo ornament. Spouts were also ornamental, formed in a pleasing curve, often fluted in the swan-neck shape, while the handle might consist of a double scroll.

Although the cost of tea was high, the beverage was an obsessive requirement by the 1760s, and its amazing popularity brought further demands for tea equipage. Despite the introduction of Sheffield plate, the very affluent still preferred sterling silver, and the numbers who could aspire to it were growing since the old hand methods of working silver were beginning to be replaced by less expensive mechanised techniques. Fortuitously for silversmiths, such techniques coincided with a new influence in fashion: neo-classical inspired outlines and ornament. The shapes of teapots now became straight-sided and because of this could be simply produced from less expensive, thin silver, rolled to a fine gauge by the improved rolling-mill. Although costs were thus reduced, the vessels produced lost none of their visual attraction because shapes were beautifully proportioned and elegant. The new fashion called for delicate engraving of foliate bands, bows, rams' heads, the key pattern, running floral scrolls, swags of foliage or cloth and laurel wreaths. Bases of teapots were flat and shapes could be circular, oval or polygonal. A silver stand on four moulded feet would be placed beneath the pot because of its

Above: teapot by Francis Crump, London, 1772.

Left: five-piece tea and coffee set by R. and S. Hennell, 1809.

flat base, but by the turn of the nineteenth century the tray had diminished in fashion and the feet appeared on the pot itself. Sometimes the marks of teapots and stands are different because they were not generally bought together. A graceful urn-shaped pot, standing upon a stem with a foot-rim, was also popular.

Towards the final years of the eighteenth century tea services began to appear, generally consisting of a teapot, milk jug, sugar bowl and matching hot-water jug and, after about 1800, a coffee pot might also be included. Designs by now had become more varied and decoration was often over-elaborate, both tendencies growing as the years progressed. The diversity of shapes later included one form of teapot with a strange – at that time – peaked front, a curvaceous oblong body, standing upon a low foot-rim. Others might be heavily embossed, displaying the revived rococo influence which dominated many. Gadrooning, too, was popular. The over-indulgence of this period, manifesting itself in varied shapes and decoration, continued until the young Queen Victoria came to the throne, when the teapot, like all other pieces, was subject to the many revived styles already described in chapter 3.

Tea kettles

It always seems a pity that the tea kettle is no longer required in the making of tea, and indeed has not been for generations since it was succeeded by the tea urn during the last 25 years or so of the eighteenth century, for it was among the most magnificent of all rococo domestic silver. Its introduction was born of the necessity for a constant supply of hot water to replenish the tiny Queen Anne teapots already discussed. The brewing of tea was a fashionable ritual in those distant days, the mistress of the house attending to it herself usually in the drawing room or salon.

Tea service for use at breakfast, Birmingham, 1904.

Early tea kettles were extremely plain and homely vessels, and their rotund shape was similar to that of the pear-shaped teapot. Likewise their spouts were of the swan-neck variety, and their lids usually topped with a wooden knop. Handles were of the swing type with wooden grips, but these varied. The flat base of the tea kettle stood upon a plain or pierced ring incorporated, with a spirit lamp, in the accompanying three-legged stand. From the legs rose a horizontal curved framework which contained the small ring for the lamp. Attached to each side of the stand there might be a pair of handles so that, once the kettle had been filled, the whole apparatus could be carried by a servant into the drawing room or boudoir for the lady of the house to infuse the precious leaves.

During successive years the shapes and styles of the kettle mirrored those of the teapot, sometimes being identical except for capacity, in which case the swing handle might be replaced by the vertical scroll-shaped type which was then popular on teapots. Occasionally the shining silver tea kettle occupied a place of particular splendour upon its own silver tripod table which stood about 30 inches high. By about the 1730s the globular teapot was joined by a globular-shaped tea kettle, and at this time the homely kettle began to appear in a more glamorous form, its contours becoming embossed with ornament also chased in high relief typical of rococo decoration, incorporating foliate and flower sprays, shells, scrolls, sometimes Oriental figures and cherubs, with the now-familiar figure of the Chinaman often taking up residence on the summit of the ornate lid. The sides of swing handles had become elaborately scrolled and the curving handle-grip covered with cane or leather. Likewise the stand was often a splendid piece of fantasy, at its more restrained incorporating cherubs' heads and scrolls, and at its most opulent perhaps designed around figures of a sea god and marine mythology.

Tea kettle and stand by Charles Kandler, London, 1727-37.

The splendour increased and the tea kettle became positively encrusted with ornament, although its expense and decoration belied the fact that it was often produced from thinly-rolled silver made possible by the new rolling-mill. Produced concurrently with these magnificent pieces were also kettles of less pretentious appearance, which were therefore less expensive since they could be made in a shorter time. By the 1740s the silver kettle might also assume an inverted-pear shape, with the body decorated in the usual rococo manner. Its popularity in one form or another was maintained for the next 15 to 20 years, until it was joined by a new design which sounded the death knell for the tea kettle. The usurper was a utilitarian vessel with a far bigger capacity than the kettle, the top of which was narrower than the wide base, with the sides sloping gently outwards. This vessel was equipped with the usual cane-covered handle but, instead of a spout, incorporated a long horizontal tap near its base. This was far more practical when larger quantities of water were required because it eliminated the tilting of the kettle for pouring. This redesigned kettle superseded the usual form and, since it was halfway to the shape and principle of the tea urn, was itself shortly eclipsed by this vessel.

Tea urns

Despite its size, the large, capacious tea urn was generally an elegant apparatus. Emerging as it did during the neo-classical period, it was usually based on the vase shape in one form or another, and stood upon a graceful stemmed foot, the end of the tap often delightfully cast and chased as an animal or bird. There were two main methods of keeping the water hot, apart from the lamp-heated urn which is believed to have been used for drawing off tea into cups and not for simply heating the water. One method used a red-hot cylindrical box-iron, inserted into a socket inside the urn, around which the water circulated to retain heat; the other involved the use of charcoal inserted into a perforated container at

Tea urn decorated with floral and foliate ornament made in 1766 by I*B.

the base, from which hot air rose through a tube inside the urn, and came out through the finial.

Certain earlier urns had squat, pear-shaped bodies, perhaps embossed with scrolls and incorporating an ornamental cartouche for the owner's crest. Scroll handles completed the style, the moulded silver spouts being similarly decorated. A ball-shaped urn appeared towards the final years of the eighteenth century, being generally either plain or fluted. During the last ten years or so a machine-like specimen appeared, known as the tea and coffee machine, which was made more commonly in Sheffield plate. It comprised separate tea, coffee and water containers and sometimes a slop basin. The water container, in reality a central urn for hot water, was roughly twice the capacity of the tea and coffee containers situated on either side of it. The hot water urn swivelled to each side so that the two smaller vessels could be replenished without being moved. Each urn or container was separately portable, but the three were based upon a tray or platform standing upon four feet. Tea urns made during the nineteenth century followed the general tendency of diversity in design and ornament.

Tea canisters or caddies

Tea was a precious commodity because of its high cost, and the very small size of early canisters reflected this when they were introduced during the final years of the seventeenth century. It is thought that the shape of the early silver tea canister imitated the shape of the Oriental stoppered jars of porcelain then being imported, because they looked rather like metal jars with a flat, rectangular base, and undecorated straight sides which curved in at the shoulders to a circular neck fitted with a slip-on, rounded cap. A late seventeenth century example might be only three inches high, but by Queen Anne's reign they were generally taller. More varied examples quickly followed, perhaps hexagonal or octagonal, sometimes triangular, occasionally decorated, reaching a height of about five inches and with an approximate capacity of four to six ounces. All were charming if quaint. In certain examples there might be a sliding section instead of a lift-off lid, but generally the version with a circular neck and rounded high cap – sometimes used to measure out the tea – continued to be made until well after the mid-eighteenth century.

Canisters were commonly made in sets of two or three for various kinds of tea: green, bohea or hyson. The records preserved by Twinings for the period list 18 different descriptions of tea, including Congoe with Pekoe, Bohea with Pekoe, Bloom Green, etc. The set of canisters would be kept in a fine wooden box, probably covered with shagreen, tortoiseshell, leather or mother-of-pearl and fitted with a lock so that the expensive tea leaves could not be pilfered by dishonest servants. Sometimes the third canister or container would be used for sugar, particularly later in the eighteenth century. Canisters were also made separately but it was not until the last few years of the eighteenth century that they became known as caddies, the word, it is thought, originating from *kati,* a Malay weight.

An Oriental vase-shaped canister appeared during the third decade of the eighteenth century, beautifully decorated with flowing scrolls, flowers

Left: tea caddy by Thomas Ash, 1710. It is engraved with 'a Talbot's head erased and collared'.

Below: tea caddy, one of a pair, showing chinoiserie decoration at its most fanciful and ingenious by T. Freeman and J. Marshall, London, 1764.

and leaves in fine repoussé work. By approximately the 1750s the *bombé* outline, popular also on furniture at that time, became fashionable. This outline consisted of a swollen upper part rising in a gradual curve from a very low waist. Some canisters of this type stood upon cast feet, perhaps shaped as volutes or acanthus leaves, while others had a base rim. General ornament was typically rococo, with a finial on the lid cast as a shell, pineapple or Chinaman. Towards the end of the 1760s this ebullient rococo ornament bowed to the simple lines of its successor. Neo-classical canisters were entirely different for they were nearly twice the size of their original predecessors, and their classical beauty was marred in no way by the mass-production methods then coming into their own.

The variety of Adam or neo-classical caddies was wide. During the last three decades or so of the eighteenth century, silversmiths excelled at these beautifully-proportioned containers. One of the most favoured shapes was a simple box caddy. These might be square, rectangular or hexagonal, and bright-cut, or perhaps simply engraved with neo-classical motifs. Their hinged lids, often with a lock, were topped by a decorative cast finial. The caddy based on the vase form was an elegant shape, embossed in low relief with classical ornament, with in-curving shoulders complemented by a decorative domed lid incorporated in the vase outline. Diversity of design was typical of the Regency years during

the following century, and particularly popular was revived rococo with
embossed chinoiseries. An oval shape was also much favoured both
during the last two or three decades of the eighteenth century and the
nineteenth century.

Left: neo-classical tea
caddy, 1773.

Below: two Sheffield
plate neo-classical tea
caddies made in 1780.

Milk and cream jugs

For many years tea was commonly drunk clear in the Chinese fashion and because of this and other reasons it is difficult to find a jug made earlier than the first few years of the eighteenth century. Early examples are in the pyriform shape, with a scrolled handle, sometimes positioned at a right-angle to the lip or spout. Diminutive cream jugs, standing no more than three inches high, were generally left undecorated, though others might have two rows of moulding at their waist. Both were made of a thick gauge metal and were weighty, despite their small size. In time the jug became more general, hammered up from the flat, with the cast spout and handle now opposite each other, standing upon a spreading moulded foot, and still with attractive scroll handles.

This simple type of jug continued unchallenged in fashion for many years. It was joined during the 1730s by an elegant form based on the helmet-shaped water ewer, scaled down to the smaller proportions of a milk jug and resembling an inverted helmet. It was hammered up from the flat, including the lip, but the handle was cast separately and soldered to the main body. It stood on a spreading moulded foot or three cast feet. The latter idea was well-liked and before long appeared on the ordinary little pyriform jug, the cast feet being hoof- or scroll-shaped, giving a new elegance to this prosaic vessel. Where legs joined the main vessel, appropriate contemporary decoration would be applied and the knees of the legs would also be enhanced by similar motifs. Jugs were either quite plain or chased or embossed with rococo scrolls, shells, flowers and pastoral scenes, often enveloping the entire surface.

Top: helmet-shaped milk jug, *circa* 1765.

Above: embossed pear-shaped jug upon three feet, *circa* 1760.

The cow-shaped jug intrigues many collectors. It appeared during the last three decades or so of the eighteenth century, the animal being made in sections and then soldered together. The jug was filled through a hole in its back, and its curled tail served as a handle. When tilted, the milk poured out through the cow's mouth. John Schuppe, a London silversmith who worked as a craftsman from 1753 to 1773, was particularly renowned for producing these strange jugs, but they were also made by other silversmiths and have been copied in successive years.

Other shapes included a pleasing boat-shaped jug, probably intended for cream rather than milk; a barrel jug which was also copied profusely in ceramics and which appeared during the 1760s; and graceful urn and vase forms of the neo-classical period. The bodies of these tapered to the base, and an elegant stem joined the base to the foot which was perhaps circular or oval and often mounted on a four-sided plinth. The handle swept up from the base to the rim in a recurving outline. These jugs, produced from thin silver, were usually made in two pieces and joined by solder to the separate foot, and were commonly decorated with bright-cutting or engraving. A far less elegant shape in fashion during the last years of the eighteenth century had a wide, oval body on a flat base, a loop handle rising from the rim and a narrow, everted spout.

During the first few years of the nineteenth century the oval jug stood upon four spherical feet, and after about 1820 the feet became decorative scrolls, the jug being lower and more squat in shape, often heavily-embossed with naturalistic decoration. Inexpensive cream jugs, made from thinly-rolled silver of flimsy quality, were produced in large quantities and often such specimens have been dented, broken and badly repaired over the years. By the time Queen Victoria ascended the throne the pear-shaped jug had been re-introduced but, since its general lines were more angular with the rounded lower half nipped in to a sharp waist and the portion beneath the waist far shorter, the gentle curves of the eighteenth century pear shape were entirely lost. Even the charm of the ornate scroll handles, which had played an important role in the design of the earlier jugs, was usually overwhelmed by a plethora of decoration, as was the entire vessel. Very popular also were the melon shape and Gothic-inspired outlines.

Sugar boxes, sugar bowls and sugar baskets

The British have not always been a sweet-toothed nation. According to G. M. Trevelyan, the country only consumed a mere 10,000 tons of sugar, even as late as 1700, although she had prosperous sugar colonies of her own. By the turn of the nineteenth century the position had altered drastically, the figure having risen to 150,000 tons. As Trevelyan points out, allowing for the population to have doubled, the average use of sugar by each person had risen seven and a half times during the eighteenth century. As might be expected the production of containers for the sweetener increased proportionately. The forerunners of the sugar bowl were exquisite sugar boxes – sometimes probably used for sweetmeats as well – which were generally oval or scallop-shaped, rather shallow, with a hinged lid, standing upon four decorative cast feet. Such examples, most of which date from the late seventeenth and very early eighteenth centuries, are rare and fetch high prices. They were followed by the hemispherical covered sugar bowl, which was very similar in shape to the porcelain tea bowls being imported from China, and which stood upon a moulded ring base and were not, or hardly at all, decorated. The loose cover, with a ring in its centre, was probably put to some use, possibly to hold tea spoons, since in those days it was quite customary to sip tea from the saucer. Small spoon trays were made during the eighteenth century to hold tea spoons.

Below left: sugar or sweetmeat box with coiled handle and over-all lobed pattern upon conch-shell shaped feet, 1676.

Below right: sugar box, *circa* 1720.

By the 1730s ornament had appeared on sugar bowls – at that time referred to as sugar dishes – including low chasing and engraving. By the middle of the century *bombé*-shaped bowls with a matching ringed cover had come into fashion, joined later by a squat vase shape which was ornately embossed, the cover ring being replaced by a finial frequently in the form of the familiar pineapple, the symbol of hospitality. This shape was far less graceful than the neo-classical vase outline which became popular from around the 1770s and which tapered gracefully to its stem upon a round foot. On either side of the shoulders of this elegant bowl were handles linked across the vessel with a series of Adam swags or bows, the high-domed lid being topped by an ornamental finial. These bowls might also be pierced.

The covers or the lids of sugar bowls had already begun to be less important and were omitted altogether in new designs, one of which was the elliptical, boat-shaped sugar basket, set upon a short stem and foot-rim, which was popular from around 1780. These were made in two designs: either from a sheet of silver in the normal way, decorated with classical motifs, or pierced and containing a blue-glass liner. The elliptical, boat-shaped design has been copied extensively ever since, and small wonder since both types of decoration are so attractive. The simple little sugar bucket, too, might be pierced with a glass liner and was sometimes made *en suite* with a similar cream pail or bucket. The sugar

Two cream pails both by Walter Brind: left, 1764; right, 1768.

Two sugar baskets: left, by William Vincent, 1771; right, by Thomas Foster, 1769.

bucket was occasionally also found in cases with tea caddies, as were silver sugar boxes or containers, the former matching the caddies but usually with larger lids. A flint-glass bowl generally superseded these.

Sugar bowls made during the final years of the eighteenth century included an oval shape with a flat base, often forming part of the growing number of tea services then becoming available, the other pieces in the tea service being of uniform style; and later a melon shape, as well as many diverse outlines typical of Regency and Victorian ideas. The sculptor, John Bell, designed a tea and coffee service which was made in electro-plate by Broadhead and Atkin in 1849. The name of the design for this service was Anthea, and the sugar basin was decorated with the plant of the sugar cane, while at the Great Exhibition of 1851 Elkingtons showed a Gothic-style service, the sugar basin of which closely resembled an ecclesiastical vessel. At the International Exhibition in 1862, one of the more important items displayed by Dixons of Sheffield was a tea and coffee service in the Grecian style, based on the vase shape and decorated with bands of palmette, fluting and the key pattern. The sugar basin in this service closely resembled its neo-classical predecessor of nearly 100 years before.

Caddy spoons

Caddy spoons have long been avidly collected, and certainly the numerous styles and designs in which they were made vary enough to suit most tastes. They were produced in large numbers from approximately the last decade or so of the eighteenth century. Early tea canisters which had round, domed caps did not need a caddy spoon since, as has been mentioned, the cap was often used to measure the tea into the pot. When these small caps were superseded by larger lids, some sort of

small ladle or spoon was required for the job. Gradually a small spoon with a short stem evolved and was kept in the canister with the tea. The bowl of the spoon was commonly in the shape of a shell, originating possibly from the fact that large sea-shells intended for use as ladles had often been packed in tea-chests by the Chinese. The caddy spoon as we know it did not appear in any great quantity before approximately 1790, but by the end of the century thousands were being produced in Birmingham, where silversmiths specialised in small objects. This trend continued for the following 50 years or more.

Collectors of caddy spoons should remember that these should usually be hallmarked. Despite their small size they were not among the items weighing less than five pennyweights which were exempt from hallmarking in 1790. The only exceptions are generally those made from filigree work. Although most will have the mark of origin of the Birmingham Assay Office (an anchor), others were also made in Sheffield, London, York, Exeter, Chester and Glasgow. Caddy spoons were also made in Ireland but these were usually larger. Watch out for badly-repaired examples, since many of the more delicate spoons snapped at the place where the stem joins the bowl, and repairs were not always as expert as they might have been.

In spite of the wide diversity of shape and ornament, caddy spoons can generally be dated by their style, or the way in which they were made, or by decoration. Earlier examples were far more delicate than their Victorian successors which were commonly cast in heavy designs, more elaborately decorated and often with complicated handles, perhaps in the shape of figures. Late eighteenth century silversmiths produced some fine examples which must rank among the highest calibre of their craft. Whether painstakingly engraved or delicately bright-cut, the technique

Birmingham caddy spoons. Centre: small chased circular bowl with snake handle, Matthew Linwood, 1807; left to right: hooded shell with ivory handle, John Lawrence and Co, 1809; engraved scoop bowl with hollow King's pattern handle, Taylor and Perry, 1835; 'bread pan' with stained wood handle, J. H. (incised), 1822; die-stamped shovel with ivory handle, Joseph Willmore, 1818; plain shovel with mother-of-pearl handle, Samuel Pemberton, 1804.

was generally carried out with infinite skill, which is why collectors will always delight in caddy spoons.

They were made in various ways. Sometimes the bowl might be die-struck, the handle pressed and then joined to the bowl by solder; while others were stamped in a single piece or cast. The bowls of very early examples might be hammered up from the flat. Some took the form of silver-mounted conical conus-shells or mussel-shells. There were those of filigree and simulated filigree, and others which were simply pierced like tea strainers. Others might be gilded. Many with their bowls shaped as silver shells were produced profusely in varying styles. Quite often they were among the earlier examples, perhaps late eighteenth century or early nineteenth century, although heavy cast shell-shaped caddy spoons were produced well into the Victorian era. Among coveted designs is the eagle's wing, the handle of which is shaped as the bird's neck, terminating with its head, and the bowl composed of beautifully-embossed 'feathers'. Joseph Willmore, Matthew Linwood and Joseph Taylor were among the Birmingham silversmiths who made these. Georgian examples date from the end of the eighteenth and early years of the nineteenth century, and their popularity continued well into the Victorian era. Their hallmarks were punched behind the stem, beneath the bowl, or sometimes among the feathers.

The jockey cap is a design which is seen frequently since it has been copied many times over the years. It is much prized by collectors who usually prefer the hallmarks to be punched on the visor, which is the handle. Make sure that hallmarks are of the right period, if you think the rest of the spoon looks genuine, because reproductions will have modern marks (see chapter 4). Some jockey caps are fairly plain, perhaps

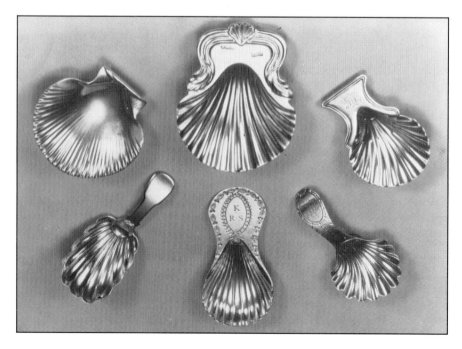

Miscellaneous shell caddy spoons.

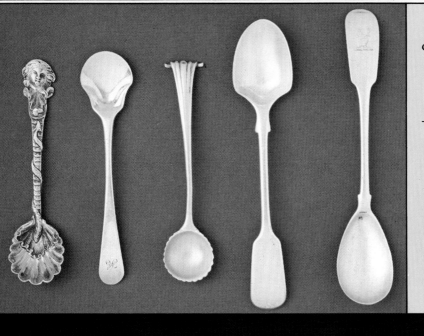

Left
Salt spoons, left to right: cast with a shell bowl, 1845; shovel-shaped bowl, *circa* 1781; fluted bowl with Onslow stem terminal, 1805. Egg spoons, *circa* 1781 and 1829.

Below
Scent bottles with silver tops, left to right: spiral, 1889; man in the moon, Birmingham, 1896; snake with garnet, Birmingham, 1901.

Top left
Left: tumbler cup by
Richard Richardson,
Chester, 1742; right:
foxhead stirrup cup by
Edward Robinson, 1806.

Centre left
Rococo coffee pot by J.
Shruder, London, *circa*
1749.

Bottom left
Fish slice and fork, *circa*
1900.

Below
King's pattern spoon,
London, *circa* 1837.

Top left
Electro-plated tea service designed by Christopher Dresser for J. Dixon and Sons, 1880.

Centre left
Brushes, left to right: Art Deco hairbrush, 1934; silver-backed hairbrush, Birmingham, 1914; whisk, London, 1912.

Bottom left
Silver photograph frames, 1898-1909.

Below
Left to right: skewer, 1801; sauce ladle, 1800; soup ladle, 1774; King's pattern sauce ladle, 1851; marrow scoop, *circa* 1750.

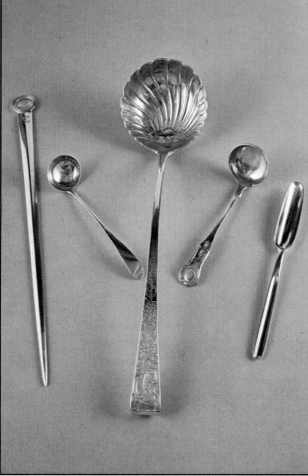

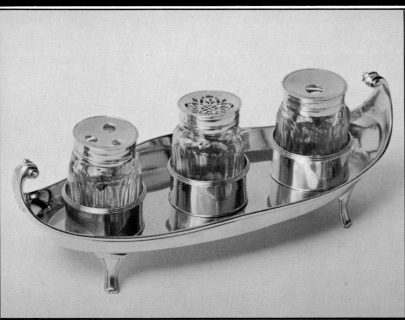

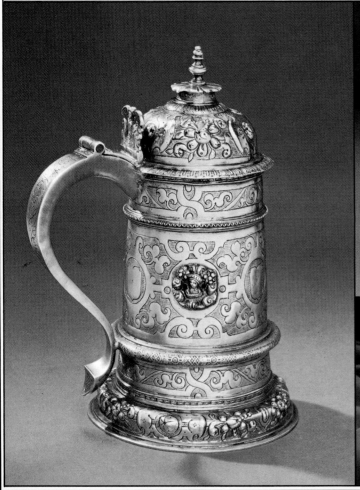

Left
George III silver-gilt inkstand by Robert Hennell, 1789.

Bottom left
Important Elizabeth I tankard, the Heddington tankard, maker's mark IR, London, 1602.

Below
George IV covered jug with repoussé decoration and cast handle, by Paul Storr, London, 1821.

Bottom right
Rectangular silver casket by Omar Ramsden, 1929.

engraved or bright-cut on the visor, while others may have a ribbed cap and peak or be engraved all over with a simple pattern. There are, as well, those which are die-stamped and decorated with geometric patterns.

Apart from the jockey cap, other popular caddy spoon designs include the leaf shape, particularly the vine leaf, the handle resembling a vine tendril in silver wire and the bowl forming the vine leaf. Others may have ribbed leaves, sometimes with finely-chased veins and also with a stalk handle of twisted wire. Leaves might be die-stamped or cast and made of silver-gilt filigree, ordinary filigree and simulated filigree. In addition to definite shapes there were those which were formed as domestic utensils such as a shovel, scoop or circular frying-pan. Handles were not always of silver, but were sometimes made of ivory, mother-of-pearl or stained wood. Running concurrently with such designs were quite simple examples and those with their bowls following a more or less general form but intricately decorated.

Various makers were famous for caddy spoons. They included, apart from those already mentioned, Samuel Pemberton (Birmingham), Hester Bateman and her family (London), Cocks and Bettridge (Birmingham), Thomas Watson and Peter Lambert (Newcastle), James le Bass and John Osborn (Dublin), William Cunningham (Edinburgh), George Fenwick (Edinburgh), George Unite (Birmingham), Edward Farrell (London), and John Foligno (London). Caddy spoons were made in abundance until around the 1860s when their popularity decreased, although, of course, certain numbers have always been produced, sometimes in new designs, but more often copies of originals. It is when such copies are resold that the collector needs to be on his guard since, although they are in no way meant to be fakes, having acquired a little age, they may appear older than they actually are. Also there is quite a vogue at the present time for producing sterling silver copies of objects which have proved popular in the past, among them caddy spoons. These generally appear in the windows of jewellers who also sell modern silver. Even if one does not wish to build up a collection devoted entirely to caddy spoons, one of these delightful old spoons is worth owning for its beauty and workmanship. A sturdier type may be put to one or two light uses at the tea table occasionally, providing it is treated carefully. For those who might become addicted, however, there are others like you who belong to the Society of Caddy-Spoon Collectors, an organisation devoted to assisting its members and to promoting the study of a delightful memento of a gracious era.

Mote skimmers and tea strainers

Although the tea strainer was among the numerous pieces of domestic silver which did not generally make their appearance until the very final years of the eighteenth century and beginning of the nineteenth century, the English tea table was not devoid of a utensil for a similar purpose. The tea strainer bore little resemblance to this predecessor and can in no way be said to be a development of it, unlike so many other items which evolved into utensils which we use today. Its forerunner was an extraordinary little implement called the mote skimmer, which was

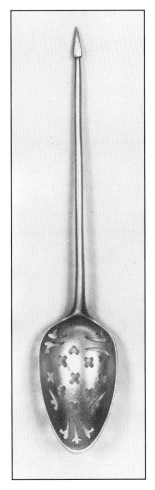

Mote skimmer, maker's mark WC, London, 1765.

usually a little longer than a tea spoon. Its bowl was pierced in a simple pattern and its rounded, slender tapering stem ended in a point. The pierced bowl was used to skim off foreign matter from the tea, hence its name, from mote, meaning particle of dust or unwanted matter. The bowl became slightly more ornate over the years, usually with a basic pattern comprised of crosses and scrolls. The pointed stem also had a use and was applied to the perforations in the teapot spout so that these would remain unblocked.

The mote skimmer played an important role in Georgian tea equipage and was sometimes sold *en suite* with tea spoons. Many are still in existence. They are recorded as early as the last years of the seventeenth century and were described variously in the eighteenth century as long tea spoons, strainer spoons and stirrer spoons, while today they are also known as mote spoons. It is unusual to find a fully-hallmarked mote skimmer, since many early skimmers bear only a maker's mark and the lion's head erased, or a maker's mark and a lion passant on later examples. Often the marks are difficult to determine since the shape of the tapering stem prevented the marks from being satisfactorily punched.

Over the years there has been controversy concerning the purpose of the mote skimmer. One theory was that the pointed or barbed end was used for spearing olives, like a similar spoon used on the Continent, or for spearing lemon or orange pips in punch, or even for use as shellfish spoons, but various references to these enigmatic tools mention them in connection with tea and this has come to be generally accepted. In early examples the back of the perforated bowl was strengthened by a rat-tail stretching from the stem, and the piercings of the bowl usually consisted of simple, circular holes. Georgian examples later replaced the rat-tail at the back of the bowl with a droplet or shell, or both, or some similar contemporary motif. Mote skimmers the size of very large table spoons are sometimes seen, often being quite heavy in weight and having George III hallmarks. These were probably used in conjunction with tea urns. Others have been noted with a marrow spoon handle instead of a barbed point, and measuring around seven inches in length. These, it is thought, were an adaptation of the tea mote skimmer for general culinary skimming. Also in circulation are bogus mote skimmers, adapted from ordinary tea spoons, but these can be distinguished from the authentic article by their generally shorter length.

Sugar nippers and sugar tongs

Unlike the mote skimmer, which has no use today but which is of interest because of its curiosity value, sugar tongs not only reflect contemporary decorative styles but can be of use at the tea table today. While prices of certain tongs have increased a good deal over recent years, nineteenth century examples may still be bought for reasonable sums. The shape of early sugar nippers was derived from contemporary fire tongs, and they commonly have baluster stems, and circular or shell-shaped grips. Some grips had rat-tail terminals at the back for strengthening, the stems sometimes being decorated with an acorn or some other decorative shape at their centre point. Early eighteenth century sugar nippers were

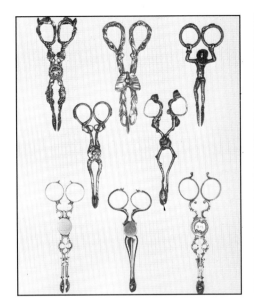 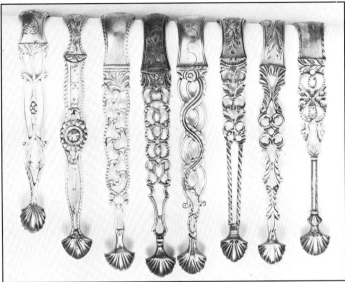

generally based on the design of scissors, however, with generous, circular handles and scrolled stems, their grips sometimes in the form of claws or shells. An unusual scissor-shaped nipper is formed like a stork, hinged through the eye, the body chased to appear like feathers and the ends of the legs looped for handles. This eighteenth century design was copied during the following century.

After about the late 1760s the bow-shaped form commonly used today was introduced, although examples of this shape were known far earlier. Bow-shaped tongs were made in three main parts with cast arms and a plain bow, and the sections were then joined by solder, the bow having previously been hammered to impart a springy quality. Later examples were made in a single strip of metal. They were variously decorated, those which were made during the neo-classical period possessing great charm, particularly when produced during the last ten years or so of the century, when they might be delicately engraved or decorated with bright-cutting. Arms might also be pierced and the grips might be shaped as shells, claws or acorns.

Tongs made after the turn of the nineteenth century were often given fiddle-shaped spoon grips, complementing the fiddle-shaped flatware of that time. These tended to be far larger than the more fragile eighteenth century examples, and were mostly left undecorated. The plain, heavier bow-shaped tongs were made for several decades, but running concurrently with these were smaller ones sold *en suite* with the silver sugar bowl. Scissor-shaped tongs enriched with cast foliate motifs were also produced, sometimes in silver-gilt, with their grips formed as a decorative leaf or other shape. Earlier nippers are seldom found to be fully hallmarked. Bow-shaped tongs, too, may not always bear a full contingent of marks since the more delicate ones often snapped and, in their repair, certain marks may have been obliterated.

Above left: sugar nippers, *circa* 1750–60, with the exception of the top row, left to right: George IV nippers with cast fruiting vines and leaf grips, by William Eley, 1827; early Victorian nippers cast with flowing scrolls, leaves and tendrils with the hinge modelled over as a butterfly, by Joseph Willmore, Birmingham, 1840; early Victorian nippers cast as a harlequin holding up two ring handles chased as snakes, by Joseph Willmore, Birmingham, 1839.

Above right: George III sugar tongs with fine pierced and decorative work, all made between *circa* 1765 and *circa* 1775.

10 | General Table Silver

Coffee pots and chocolate pots

Coffee was first introduced into England during the third decade of the
seventeenth century. By the later years of the century so many coffee
houses had been opened that in 1675 Charles II issued a proclamation for
their suppression since certain London coffee houses had become places of
intense political activity and intrigue. However, the proclamation was
quickly withdrawn because it caused such an outcry. Coffee houses
usually made a cover charge of a penny and twopence ($\frac{1}{2}$p and 1p) for a
dish of coffee, while retail prices of the beverage, as recorded by Twinings
in 1717, varied from approximately five to six shillings (25p to 30p) a
pound. The entries in the ledger do not describe any particular type of
coffee, but mention 'slack' and 'high', meaning light or dark roast. In the
home it was customary to grind the coffee beans in an ordinary coffee mill
which might cost a few shillings.

The silver coffee pot by this time was already a fairly elegant vessel and
would be found quite often in the homes of noblemen and the wealthy.
There were two main shapes. The more usual type had a straight
tapering body with a shallow moulded foot, and a hinged cover with a
rounded dome surmounted by a finial, and was made in various shapes
including circular and polygonal; the other was based on the pear shape
and is often associated with Huguenot coffee pots. Spouts were
occasionally positioned at right-angles to the handle. Straight spouts
soon gave way to the charm of the swan-neck variety, which sometimes
sported a hinged cap at the end, in accordance with contemporary teapots.
Ornament included cut-card work, perhaps around the base of the pot
where it might be applied to a gadrooned foot-rim, or where the spout or
handle joined the body. Covers were often attractively fluted. Other
examples were left undecorated or were simply engraved with a
coat-of-arms. Decorated rococo coffee pots assumed much of the ornament
associated with this period, perhaps chased with cupids or scrolls or
embossed with foliage and flowers. In certain examples the foot-rim
might be replaced by three decorative feet, and the short spout was
sometimes shaped as an eagle's head.

The usual type of neo-classical coffee pot popular during the last three
decades of the eighteenth century was based on the vase shape, which
stood upon a moulded spreading foot, its lid topped with a finial often in
the shape of an urn. Decoration included shallow fluting, acanthus

Far left: chocolate pot, 1703.

Left: coffee pot by Paul de Lamerie, 1738.

leaves, rams' heads, running floral scrolls and swags of foliage or ribbon bows. Moulding was common and might consist of beading, astragals and reeding. Other contemporary decoration was also used.

Victorian coffee pots, often made *en suite* with a tea set, might have a plain round body and scroll handle, or incorporate various cyclic ornament including naturalistic and Gothic motifs, the former featuring the popular vine plant and the latter stylised trefoils. Many were made in the fashionable revived neo-classical style.

The silver chocolate pot followed the popular styles of coffee pots, but with one distinction. This was a small, covered opening in the lid into which a swizzle stick would be placed for stirring the chocolate to an even consistency. Chocolate pots also followed the fashionable styles adopted by hot-water jugs, and some particularly fine neo-classical examples were produced at the time this style became more general.

Cake and fruit baskets

Early pierced baskets were heavy, magnificent pieces but these are rare. Eighteenth century examples were oval, rectangular or circular with a flat base and ornately-pierced sides, often featuring two small cabled silver handles which were later superseded by the swing type. Huguenot silversmiths were much acclaimed for their fine pierced and embossed baskets, and superb examples of their work, which clearly show why they were so admired, can be seen in various stately homes and museums.

However, some of their achievement must also be attributed to the
English invention of the rolling-mill which had been improved by 1728,
allowing the production of a fine gauge silver for more complicated
piercing. London silversmiths also made many fine table baskets. From
approximately the end of the 1730s a shaped and pierced 'skirt' which
incorporated cast rococo ornament concealed the base. Later baskets had
four decorative feet. Among the numerous early eighteenth century
patterns for table baskets were those which incorporated finely-pierced
diamonds and circles, with the rim decorated by appliqué and probably
edged with beading.

Paul de Lamerie, one of the most distinguished Huguenot craftsmen,
produced some superlative baskets featuring incredibly intricate work.
Sometimes the piercing was so fine that it resembled delicate
wicker-work, but he also produced complex rococo forms in an elaborate
pattern. Other baskets of his take the form of large scallop-shells,
perhaps fluted or pierced, with delightful shell-shaped rims. Such baskets
might stand on dolphin shapes or deliciously ornate feet. Inspired work of
this category was sometimes copied by lesser silversmiths, though the
baskets produced during the rococo period are generally of a very high
standard, and there is much to admire in the vigorous decoration and
workmanship. From about 1740 silversmiths increasingly raised the
body of the basket from one sheet of silver. Everted rims were enlarged in
size, ornately decorated with appliqué work, and shaped in such a way
that the beautiful patterns of pierced work inside the basket could be
easily observed. The patterns would be based on intricate designs of
scrolls, circles, crescents, quatrefoils and so on, cleverly varied in size and
grading. Sometimes pierced panels would be intermingled with solid
ones.

Above left: cake basket
by John le Sage, 1741.

Above right: rare cheese
dish by Edward Wakelin,
London, *circa* 1760.

Thus silversmiths working in London established a fine reputation for
baskets which were to be a major part of their work for many years. Later
they achieved the elaborate piercing by using the fly-press, which was
then able to punch small work swiftly and accurately. Mass-production
was the next step. The number of panels used in a basket increased,
sometimes incorporating as many as 20 or 30. After being soldered
together to form the sides of the basket, the joins would be concealed

beneath decorative beading or some other form of ornament; neo-classical table baskets are therefore an interesting example of the results achieved when the hand-work by craftsmen and the new factory techniques were combined. By around the last decade or so of the eighteenth century mass-production methods were becoming widely adopted and hand-work was correspondingly diminishing. The silver used was also far thinner, resulting in a general lowering of the formerly high standard.

Table baskets made of silver wire also became popular after about 1760 and stayed in fashion for the next 65 years or so. The framework of the

Silver wire-work cake basket, 1763.

basket consisted of wire decorated with hammered and chased motifs of current design, perhaps sprays of wheat, flowers or vine leaves. Silver table baskets were copied first in Sheffield plate and from the mid-nineteenth century in electro-plate, and in this way the once highly-prized possession of the nobles found its way into more modest homes. The late nineteenth and early twentieth century price for a less intricate basket in sterling silver might be around £7 16s 0d (£7.80), and £2 11s 0d (£2.55) for its counterpart in electro-plate.

Sugar casters, pepper casters and muffineers

Decorative piercing was an attractive feature of the eighteenth century caster, reflecting in general the stylistic motifs used in baskets. Early casters were made either singly, or in sets of three: two small casters for black pepper and cayenne pepper or, perhaps, dry mustard, and a larger one for sugar. The piercing in these sets matched exactly so, no matter which flavouring was required, it issued forth at a uniform rate. Sometimes the flow of cayenne pepper or dry mustard was modified by various devices including an inner lining containing smaller perforations. In other sets this caster was 'blind' with a pull-off lid. A bayonet fastener secured the lid to the body in many early examples.

Early eighteenth century casters were straight-sided, cylindrical or octagonal, baluster or pyriform. The latter was more general, and stood upon a moulded foot, while its pierced domed cover or lid was surmounted by a cast finial. Earlier examples were usually undecorated, except sometimes for a horizontal band of moulding, and their covers were of a simple pull-off type. They later became more ornate and might incorporate cut-card work. Pyriform casters were also made in octagonal form and both types remained in fashion until about 1750, during this time becoming beautifully embossed, perhaps with decorative cartouches. From around 1740 an ogee form also became popular.

The reign of George III saw the return of the cylindrical shape, now pierced with neo-classical inspired motifs, as were those with pierced sides containing blue-glass liners. Sets of six small casters were also commonly made and the vase shape generally apparent in domestic silver was introduced. Casters in this form were made abundantly for the next 20 or 30 years, and running concurrently with this type were copies of earlier examples. Casters with handles are often referred to as dredgers. Their use remains uncertain, but in all probability it was the sprinkling of spice, for which there was a positive craving during the eighteenth century. They are usually simple cylindrical objects, standing about four inches high with a bun lid which was perforated with circular holes – like pepper casters when sold separately – and only a minimum of ornament.

Another spice caster was the muffineer, which was used for sprinkling cinnamon on hot buttered toast during the later years of the eighteenth century. Although roughly the same height as the dredger, these were generally vase-shaped and did not have a handle. They, too, had a low-domed lid which was pierced with circular holes. Some were embossed or engraved, while others, usually later examples, were undecorated. They were also made with their sides decoratively pierced and containing a blue-glass liner.

Top: caster by Charles Adams, *circa* 1709.

Above: dredger, *circa* 1710.

Mustard pots

The use of mustard for culinary purposes goes back into antiquity, but it was a Mrs Clements who started mustard-making on a truly commercial scale in about 1720. She had the idea of producing a fine mustard flour which she made at 73 Saddler Street, Durham. Her method was simply to grind the seed in a mill and then to subject it to the various processes used in flour-making. Mrs Clements, who took good care to keep her secret to herself, met with instant success. George I liked it and the court followed him, establishing the preference for paste mustard which still exists today. Mrs Clements not only supplied outlets in London, travelling there twice yearly, but also the more important towns 'throughout England. Since she travelled from Durham, the fine new mustard flour became known as Durham Mustard.

But what of a silver pot in which to place it? These came into being following her discovery and had become established by the middle of the century. Early examples were drum-shaped or cylindrical, and sometimes oval or octagonal with flat, hinged lids in which a groove was left at the side for the insertion of a ladle-shaped spoon. From the early 1760s silversmiths listed tankards with hinged lids as mustard tankards, although they had been in use earlier. They were made from a sheet of silver, joined by a soldered seam beneath the handle. Lids were raised by a thumbpiece which was decoratively cast and chased. Handles were scroll or S-shaped. Moulding would usually strengthen the rim and base of the pot. Pierced examples with blue-glass liners were fashionable, being hand-pierced originally and pierced by the fly-press at a later date. The vase-shaped pot was in vogue during the last 30 years or so of the eighteenth century, as was the elliptical shape. At the end of the century, straight-sided oval pots appeared, decorated as the other forms, with beading, engraving and bright-cutting. Also making their appearance at this time were rectangular and barrel-shaped pots.

The Regency era saw the emergence of matching sets of domestic silver, and an assortment of matching salt and mustard pots now began to pour

Below left: large vase-shaped mustard pot, pierced with flowers and ferns and bright-cut with festoons, by John Lambe, London, 1786.

Below right: barrel-shaped mustard pot with handle cast and chased in the form of a grimacing monkey, by Joseph Angell II and Joseph Angell III, London, 1846.

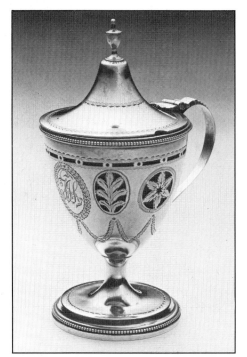

forth from manufacturing silversmiths. It was natural, then, that the cruet, with its silver or silver-mounted containers grouped together, grew in popularity. By the second and third decades of the nineteenth century, the cylindrical mustard pot was altogether heavier with thicker cast S-shaped handles, incorporating more elaborate mouldings around the rim and base. Various new shapes appeared including a compressed circular form chased with naturalistic patterns and pear-shaped pots. Hexagonal or octagonal pots were pierced or engraved.

In the early years of Queen Victoria's reign designs became most fanciful and included the bizarre, like the pot with the handle incorporating a monkey with a look of horror on its face and its tongue lolling out. Was this a device to let us know that the stuff was hot? Animal shapes and novelties abounded, from plump porkers to kittens; sometimes demure, sometimes grotesque. Among the novelties was a busby, made in 1908, crested and engraved with the motto 'I am ready', its accompanying mustard spoon having a cockade handle. Another was a riding boot with a whip-handle spoon. Among Art Nouveau pieces was one designed by C. R. Ashbee and made by the Guild of Handicraft at the turn of the century. This elegant little piece with its simple, flowing lines, tapering in towards the top, and pierced above the waist, has a slightly-domed overlapping cover, its finial set with a semi-precious stone.

Below left: spool-shaped basket-weave mustard pot with ropework base and plaited rim, by William Brown and John Cook Clark, Birmingham, 1858.

Below right: cylindrical mustard pot, engraved with fruit and formal ornament, with an infill of lozenges, by Henry and Henry Lias of H. Lias and Son, London, 1866.

Salt cellars

Few basic changes have been made to the salt cellar since the eighteenth century, and even those produced today in sterling silver or electro-plate are usually exact, or very close, copies of their predecessors. From time to time, of course, designers have endeavoured to break away from established forms, and the Victoria and Albert Museum, London, has a superb Art Nouveau specimen in parcel-gilt by C. R. Ashbee which incorporates amber and a small figure, the latter being characteristic of Ashbee's work, but this 'salt' would be considered too ornate for general use. An interesting example of 1866 by Stephen Smith was of frosted silver with figures of sowers and men carrying baskets of seeds upon their backs.

Elegant, antique salt cellars are in demand, although great care should be taken to ensure that they are cleaned properly (see chapter 7). Probably most popular of all are the neo-classical pierced versions with Bristol blue-glass liners, which show the intricate piercing in sharp relief. These have been produced since the 1760s, worked at first by hand with the fret-saw and later stamped by the fly-press, the latter method piercing considerable numbers. Always much in demand has been an oval form, standing on four decorative feet, made in either sterling silver or Sheffield plate, and of a rounded or polygonal shape. The boat-shaped

Salt cellar by William Abdy, London, 1813.

cellar, with a short stem balanced by an oval spreading foot, was typical of the neo-classical period from about 1770, and retained its popularity until around 1825. It is among the most elegant of designs and has been understandably copied ever since.

In common with the shapes of domestic vessels, a rounded oblong salt cellar on four ball feet was another prominent design from approximately 1805 until about 1820, while the variously-pierced circular, straight-sided shape with three or four feet remained in vogue until the middle of the nineteenth century and later. Victorian salt cellars, in common with other domestic items of the time, were subject to a revival of most previous styles and ornament, including rococo, Greek and Roman classicism, ancient Egyptian motifs and naturalism. The pleasing bowl or cauldron shape, which had appeared originally in about 1730, was included among such revivals. These stood upon three or four feet, including hoof and scallop shapes, and the short legs curved attractively into the bowl. The joints thus formed were decorated with lions' heads, rams' heads, cherubs and other contemporary ornament, and these were linked around the bowl by embossed swags and festoons. Victorian and Edwardian revivals range from the over-decorated to the fair copy. The ordinary, basic trencher salt was made in circular, square, triangular and octagonal shapes and was the first type of 'cellar' to emerge after the great salt fell into disuse during the seventeenth century. Such salts are among the few designs which have not been copied extensively, due no doubt to their solid appearance, although a spool shape which appeared during the reign of George I is still emulated.

Victorian parcel-gilt novelty condiment set by Robert Hennell, 1872.

Epergnes

These ornamental table pieces have undergone a revival of interest in recent years with the increased knowledge of antiques generally. Epergnes, or centrepieces as they are sometimes known, were produced in many forms, both elaborate and simple, but certainly always provided glamour at the table. They appeared during the 1720s, and one is recorded in a contemporary royal inventory as having 'one table basket and cover, one foote, four salt boxes, four small salts, four branches, six casters and four sauceboats'. This gives a rough idea how these hanging devices with a central stem and branches saved space on the table, which was their original purpose, quite apart from their ornamental value. It was probably this latter quality, however, which was responsible for their rapid growth in fashion. They became exquisitely decorated with rococo ornament and were later bedecked with all manner of classical motifs. Others were in the Chinese style with elaborate pillars and delicately-pierced pagoda roofs and baskets, with their branches in the form of recurving scrolls.

Regency épergnes might be mounted on a platform with a central pillar upon which would be set a large cut-glass dish. Four branches would support small, matching dishes, and the entire piece would be heavily decorated. Victorian examples included both magnificent and quite simple, smaller versions. The former often incorporated an amazing mixture of figures with a general theme, which might be exotically naturalistic, Gothic or classical. Sheffield plate épergnes were probably produced in more diverse patterns than any other piece of comparable domestic plated silver, manufacturers devising a stream of ideas including perhaps as many as 250 patterns with which to tempt customers during the last decade of the eighteenth century and first 15 years or so of the nineteenth. These, too, took all kinds of forms and had grown excessively ornate by Victorian days, at which time they sometimes included coloured-glass liners or bowls.

Sauceboats and tureens

Sauceboats were among the pieces of domestic silver which emerged during the second decade of the eighteenth century, possibly because George I introduced certain types of sauces to England at that time. Early examples had a pouring lip on either side of the vessel, in between which were two scroll handles. Rococo sauceboats were beautifully ornate and by the 1740s the earlier moulded base was surpassed in fashion by three or four cast feet in ornamental shapes, while the outline of the vessel evolved into an oval or *bombé* form which was concurrently in use for tureens. The delightfully elaborate scroll handle, positioned opposite the pouring lip, was one of the major attractions of the sauceboat of this period. Rims were shaped and decorated, and the actual vessel might be either undecorated or embossed with a floral pattern. Others might have a more rounded body which might be fluted to resemble a shell, a shape which reappeared again early in the nineteenth century when it was also made in Sheffield plate. Victorian sauceboats included those with rotund sides and a scalloped, gadrooned rim, three hoof feet and a scroll handle. These were made in various sizes and were often sold in sets of two, three or more.

Although tureens in the *bombé* style were not introduced until the 1740s, they were recorded at the beginning of the century, and after this time various examples came into existence. They are thought to have been of Huguenot origin, and certainly their name is thought to derive from the French *terrine.* The outlines of rococo examples were based on sweeping curves, and these were superbly decorated with cast floral and foliate ornament, masks, fruit and birds. Beautifully-proportioned neo-classical examples, commonly based on an oval shape, were among the most splendid silver produced during the last three decades of the eighteenth century. These were elegantly decorated with appropriate classical motifs, their edges commonly reeded, beaded or gadrooned and their covers embellished with radiating fluting or gadrooning. Sweeping

Below left: sauce tureen, one of a pair, struck with the mark of Boulton and Fothergill, Birmingham, 1776.

Below right: tureen and stand by Thomas Heming, London, 1776.

vertical loop handles rose from the base to the rim. Regency examples stood upon four cast feet which replaced the elegant spreading stem of the neo-classical tureen, and the graceful vertical sweep of the handles was superseded by horizontal loop handles. Certain examples, excessively decorated in a revived rococo style, might weigh as much as 100 ounces. By the final two decades of the nineteenth century, tureens, having passed through the various revivals of the Victorian era, were often surprisingly quite plain, being simply decorated by beading or gadrooning at their edges.

Cruet frames

The almost-defunct cruet frame – basic, unembellished and purely functional – which evokes memories of the older type of hotel dining-table, was a very poor relation indeed to its splendid eighteenth century counterpart. The twentieth century versions owe some of their severity to Edwardian designers who, in their search for simplicity, reacted against the plethora of Victorian ornament and perhaps went a little too far. The exquisite cruet stand first made a hesitant appearance, presenting as it did an entirely new idea for the table, during the final years of the seventeenth century and first two decades or so of the eighteenth century. It was then generally kept on the table until about 1850, after which time it was relegated to the sideboard.

These earlier frames of wire were made to contain the bottles which had become more general after George Ravenscroft's invention of 'flint' glass in about 1676. The mallet-shaped bottles were sold with little silver caps surmounted by ornamental finials and engraved with the crests, coats-of-arms, etc of their owners. The handled frame or stand was an innovation by silversmiths to hold these bottles for oil and vinegar, either as a pair or in a larger frame to include a set of three casters (called a Warwick). The idea was, not surprisingly, a big success, being simple and practical, consisting of a base upon decorative feet, supporting pierced ornamental containers, into which the bottles fitted. Impressive, double-scroll handles were soon integrated into the design of the bottles, curving from the neck of the, by now, beautifully-decorated and usually hinged cap, to the shoulders, a spout having been also incorporated into the design for ease of pouring.

By the last three decades of the eighteenth century an elliptical boat-shaped frame had become popular, as had those which were square, oval, oblong, or circular, with rounded or cut corners. Both the frames and their bottles were either extremely ornate or very simple. Designs were numerous, and a single manufacturer might have between 300 and 400 patterns in his catalogues spanning the last decade of the eighteenth century and first ten years of the next. Fine work abounded, and the bottles contained in the frames were of exquisitely-cut glass. The soy frame was also produced after about the middle of the eighteenth century, following the introduction of soy sauce some time earlier. Its vogue persisted into the nineteenth century, when a soy frame might accommodate as many as ten bottles for variously-flavoured sauces. An enormous range of Sheffield plate cruets was made simultaneously with those in sterling silver. Examples of either should contain their original bottles and, because of this, a basic knowledge of glass is essential.

Warwick cruet stand, 1747.

Mazarines, dish rings, dish crosses and cheese toasters

All of these items are among the pieces of domestic silver introduced during the eighteenth century for which we no longer have a use. The mazarine was a practical piece and was mostly required at a time when fish was generally cooked by boiling in water. It was a pierced vessel, plate or drainer which was put into a larger dish and upon which the fish would be placed so that the surplus juices would strain through into the main dish. It was probably also used for vegetables in the same way, although the piercings denote by their frequent nautical patterns that the main purpose was for draining fish.

Dish rings, also called potato rings, are generally believed to have been placed on the table to prevent plates from leaving marks on the surface of it. Another theory has it that the rings were stood upon the plate, thus making a vessel into which potatoes and other foods could be placed, but this seems unlikely. Others believe that they were ornamental stands for bowls, plates and dishes. They were nearly all made in Ireland, and were generally around three to four inches in height and approximately seven to eight inches in diameter. Their sides mostly curved inward to a waist and out again, similar to a spool, and they were often wonderful examples of a high standard of craftsmanship, showing a great love of fantasy in the complicated piercing and decoration. The latter included an incredible variety of figures – sometimes Chinese – birds, and naturalistic forms or entire pastoral scenes. Because of the fact that dish rings were among pieces of Irish silver not assayed, sometimes being punched with only the maker's mark, they are vulnerable to the techniques of the faker.

Dish ring by Richard Williams, Dublin, *circa* 1780.

Dish crosses, although no longer in use, are the sort of simple but effective idea which could usefully be revived in these times when the cost of power for heated food trolleys is on the increase. They consisted of two pairs of arms, standing upon four legs, which crossed centrally and at which point was set a spirit lamp. Each arm had a decorative bracket to support the dish and to hold it clear of the naked flame. The arms could be increased or decreased in size to take various dishes.

Cheese toasters conjure up visions of a cosy fireside scene. They were in use when the fire was the focal point of the room and declined in fashion after approximately the third decade of the nineteenth century, although one wonders why since they could have been used long after this. They appeared early in the reign of George III and were made first in silver. Later various examples were copied in Sheffield plate; sometimes the main dish might be of Sheffield plate and the toast compartments, of which there were generally six, of sterling silver. The cheese toaster consisted basically of an oblong covered pan or dish, divided into compartments or individual containers, into which was placed previously-toasted bread covered with thin slices of cheese. Beneath the individual dishes was a hot-water compartment which kept the toast warm, the water usually being poured in through the handle which was unscrewed, or via an opening in the side which had a cap. Fixed to the cover of the main dish was a chain which raised the lid while the dish was on the fire, thus reflecting the heat and causing the cheese to bubble and brown quickly.

Monteiths, punch bowls and punch ladles

The monteith, which looks like a punch bowl with an ornate rim and lifting handles, first appeared some 20 years after the Restoration but became more general during the later years of the seventeenth century and earlier years of the eighteenth. Monteiths are comparatively rare pieces, and therefore fetch high prices. Their scalloped and notched rims were generally removable. The monteith was filled with cold water, then glasses were hung by their foot upon the notches, and thus allowed to cool in the water. When the monteith was not being used in this manner it is assumed that the rim was removed and the deep bowl filled with punch. The monteith-shaped bowl for punch was revived towards the end of the nineteenth century. In the eighteenth century it was superseded by the punch bowl, an important vessel throughout this century. Early examples are usually of a heavier silver and comparatively undecorated, but as the century progressed they might be embossed with fluting, sometimes incorporating leaf and floral patterns, or embossed and chased in the rococo style. Later they were decorated with neo-classical motifs (see chapter 3).

Monteith by George Garthorne, 1687.

Accompanying the punch bowl would be a long-handled ladle, early examples being of a heavy-gauge silver, like the bowl, with their handles perhaps of turned wood, ivory or ebony. Numerous designs came into being after about 1740, including circular and oval bowls with pouring lips; bowls shaped like the popular nautilus-shell; goose-egg shapes; and those with crown pieces hammered out to form the bowl. Others simply had a coin inserted into the base, but such coins were not always contemporary.

Tankards

Although use was made of cut-card work on some tankards and certain presentation examples made during the early years of the eighteenth century, the tankard by its very nature is not generally regarded as a Huguenot vessel, since the Huguenots originated from a wine-drinking country. It was the London silversmiths, therefore, who tended to specialise in the tankard, and generally the examples which bear the marks of Huguenot makers stray a little from the true outline of the English vessel. Other ornament on late seventeenth and early eighteenth century tankards which, for the most part, were comparatively undecorated, included gadrooning, engraved coats-of-arms and occasionally more elaborate surface engraving, perhaps with chinoiseries. Shapes were simple.

Below left: tankard of silver parcel-gilt by William Ramsey, Newcastle, *circa* 1670.

Below right: tankard by John Downes, London, 1701.

The tankard in general use during Queen Anne's reign had a low-domed cover or lid and might be given a double-scroll handle and scrolling thumbpiece. A rotund or tulip-shaped form appeared at about this time, with a rounded base upon a concave moulded foot-ring, while double-domed lids became popular around the time of the accession of George I. The tankard was hammered up from the flat until roughly the third to fourth decade of the eighteenth century, from which time it became general practice to hammer up the lower part of the vessel and to make the upper section separately, joining the two parts by solder. The joint would be covered by ornamental moulding. Cromwellian tankards were mostly undecorated, except perhaps for their owner's coat-of-arms. Single, stepped lids were the vogue. Tankards became bulbous after the middle of the eighteenth century and subsequent examples were also given barrel-type bodies. More decorative post-Restoration styles might incorporate strapwork and embossed ornament. In the most part, succeeding styles and sizes were similar to preceding forms, ranging from the tall, flagon-shaped examples made in the time of Charles I to the rotund form made from about 1750.

The term 'peg' tankard owes its name to the eight pins, or pegs, spaced evenly in a vertical line inside the vessel. A cylindrical type of tankard which often had 'pegs' sometimes stood upon three pomegranate-shaped feet and incorporated either engraved tulip or lily motifs or embossed tulip and acanthus decoration. These originated from Scandinavia and were copied by English craftsmen, usually near Hull, Newcastle and York, since these towns were closest to the north coast and came under the influence of both Scandinavian and Dutch craftsmen. The pegs were an early form of measure, and, according to Doctor Pegge, the seventeenth century antiquary, 'the first person who drank was to empty the tankard to the first peg or pin, the second was to empty to the next pin, etc'. Since these tankards usually held two quarts, this allowed each person to drink the full measure of one gill or half a pint.

Top: tankard by William Shaw and William Priest, London, 1756.

Above: early George I beer jug, London, 1714.

Beer jugs

Beer was served in varying sizes of jugs, generally of a sturdy character, and often with pear-shaped bodies and scroll handles. They usually had a lid or cover, but were also made with open tops. The pouring spout was sometimes worked from the rim, while other examples featured spouts which had been made separately and soldered to the main body. Beer jugs should not be confused with covered hot-water jugs, which were usually more elegant and followed cyclic fashions in styles and decoration in order to match other pieces of domestic table silver.

Beakers and mugs

Although beakers are a primitive and ancient form of drinking vessel, in silver or silver-gilt they were scarce and, while known of in mediæval times, they did not become general until far later. Those in use during the seventeenth century were usually first shaped as a cylinder with a splayed-out top, the vertical seam being soldered and a circular base inserted – a technique which had been employed for many years. At another stage they were hammered up from the flat. They were often

fairly small, perhaps around four to six inches in height, and sometimes heavily embossed with floral patterns. Some examples are simply scratch-engraved. Certain beakers were also influenced by Scandinavian craftsmen and copies of these can sometimes be dated from about 1740 to 1775. Others, engraved and bright-cut, tapering gradually to the base, were made during the later years of the century as were reeded examples. The latter type was also produced in the nineteenth century.

Early mugs, like beakers, were either hammered up from the flat or formed into cylinders, soldered, then given a base and a handle. They· were commonly about three to six inches in height, and closely resembled contemporary tankards, but did not have lids. By the end of the seventeenth century and beginning of the eighteenth they might be chased, fluted, reeded or engraved with chinoiseries, with straight or rounded sides. Others were devoid of ornament. Just after George I came to the throne the tulip-shaped mug became fashionable, but towards the end of the eighteenth century the straight-sided mug reappeared. Those produced during the following century borrowed their shapes and ornament from all periods.

Above left: beaker, London, 1678.

Above right: William Darker mug with double-scroll handle, London, 1729, with bold chasing and texturing added *circa* 1860.

Tumbler cups and stirrup cups

Tumbler cups were simple, amusing little vessels which never actually tumbled, because the silver in their rounded base was of a heavier weight than the sides, causing them to right themselves before they spilled their contents. Thus they were most convenient in carriages when refreshment was taken, since they could be relied upon to stay more or less upright, however rough the road or unpredictable the reactions of the horses in an emergency. These tiny cups appeared from about 1650 and were much in demand thereafter, particularly during the eighteenth century. They were usually devoid of decoration except for the owner's crest or a little engraving, and measured from around two inches in height, seldom being more than four.

The stirrup cup was based on the shape of an animal's head, commonly a fox or dog and occasionally a hare and was popularly used at hunts from the last few decades of the eighteenth century to just before the middle of the nineteenth century. The stirrup cup was possibly derived from the classical *rhyton* of terracotta, and was eventually succeeded by the practical but less picturesque cylindrical saddle flask.

Strainers and wine funnels

Strainers used in the service of wine or punch were common during the eighteenth century when punch was such a favoured form of refreshment. They were described variously in contemporary catalogues as orange, lemon or punch strainers, the latter being larger. In the case of the small strainer the orange or lemon juice, which was used to flavour many types of punch, was poured through it into a separate bowl and then added to the punch. The larger version was rested on the rim of the actual punch bowl and the orange or lemon juice was poured directly into the punch through it. Strainers, which were also used for wine, were often exceedingly well-made, showing attractive piercing with either one or two flat handles soldered to the rim. Sometimes the owner's crest or initials might be engraved upon one of the handles.

The wine funnel appeared more commonly during the last four decades or so of the eighteenth century, probably because it became fashionable at about this time to decant the wine into 'flint' glass decanters, although they were in use far earlier. They might be undecorated or given an ornate rim and might be variously shaped including an urn shape or ogee, sometimes with a detachable strainer fitted at the waist. Some had a ribbed stem which permitted air bubbles to escape, or a curved tip which prevented air from entering the liquid. Others were used for pouring spirits into square decanters and had straight spouts which tapered. A great many wine funnels, like strainers, were made in Sheffield plate.

Wine tasters and brandy warmers

Wine tasters, although not a general domestic vessel, survive in sufficient quantities to make them a less rare collector's item than would be expected. They are shallow, circular vessels only about an inch in depth, sometimes less, and usually no more than approximately three inches in diameter. They were thus eminently portable which was one of their requirements since original examples were used by members of the vintners trade and sometimes by those who visited the vineyards abroad, who carried these little objects with them – a custom known since the fifteenth century at least. Vintners would also visit the wine vaults in the City of London and the little wine tasters would be of great use on these and similar occasions. Most wine tasters were made in silver because it was considered the best metal for the purpose. Some have a raised centre.

Wine taster, maker's
mark FI and wheel,
London, 1642.

They usually had a horizontal handle and sometimes two, while other handles were in the form of a simple loop or ring. Many wine tasters were undecorated or sparsely so, comprising bosses and/or gadrooning, the former being quite usual by itself in a basic pattern. Others were sometimes decorated with repoussé ornament, and eighteenth century examples particularly might be embossed with a vine motif. Watch out for later, sometimes twentieth century, souvenir-type vessels, which are often cast and perhaps incorporate a Continental type of coin, for these are not intended to be taken seriously.

Brandy warmers are diminutive, lidless saucepans, with either rounded or straight sides, everted rims and often a pouring lip, depending on the type. Most examples seen today date from the mid-eighteenth century and among them are those which are very small, perhaps under three-and-a-half inches in diameter. Hallmarks are generally to be found on the rounded, tapering handle below the wooden portion, or on the outside of the vessel below the rim.

Coasters

Coasters are much in demand, not only by collectors, but by all who appreciate the subdued glow of old silver on the dining-table. They came into more general use from approximately 1760 and were sold individually or in sets. Often described as bottle stands, their purpose was to prevent the surface of the table from becoming scratched or marked as the wine bottle was pushed along for the replenishment of the glass. The base of the coaster was usually made of boxwood, covered beneath with green baize. The beautifully pierced and embossed sides were similar to other contemporary table pieces such as salt cellars or dish rings. After about 1770 the sides were mechanically pierced. The join between the sides and the wooden base was generally disguised by some form of ornament such as reeding.

The use of coasters increased with the vogue for glass decanters, and their sides were decorated according to the fashion prevalent at the time, both pierced and solid. A great many were made in Sheffield plate, and one manufacturer's records available at the end of the eighteenth and start of the nineteenth centuries show that no less than 100 patterns had been available over a period of 25 years, few of which were priced higher

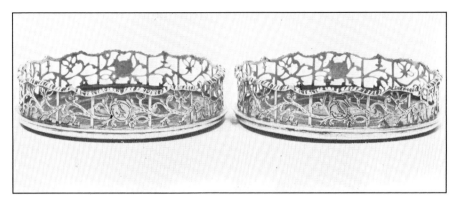

Left: wine coasters by Charles T. and George Fox in the style of the 1770s although made in London in 1847. The crested sides are pierced and engraved with stylised foliage.

Below: wine labels, late eighteenth or early nineteenth century.

than 20 shillings (£1) a pair. The Regency period saw the introduction of many intriguing and sometimes amusing designs for two bottles, some of which were aptly described as wine wagons since they were on wheels. The decoration for single coasters would include florid ornament, embossed with the vine or ivy leaf and other naturalistic forms, and perhaps rimmed with gadrooning. Others continued to be pierced.

Wine labels

Silver wine labels (bottle tickets) were made in a vast range of decorative shapes, one authority on the subject claiming that over 1,000 different names and designs had been noted over the years. Their original use was not purely ornamental, however, as it tends to be today, for they were used to identify bottles of wine, replacing the hand-written ticket which was generally attached to the pack thread on the cork. They appeared during the third decade or so of the eighteenth century when they were made by Sandilands Drinkwater and John Harvey of Gutter Lane, London. Their diversity later matched the variety of wines, cordials and miscellaneous other brews which were imbibed, consumed as a relish or applied, as in the case of eau-de-Cologne.

Very early examples mostly consisted of three shapes: a narrow oblong, crescent and escutcheon. They continued to be popular throughout following years despite the introduction of hundreds of other designs. These might be hoop-shaped, elliptical, or shaped like a vase or initial. Many were cast as vine leaves. Exquisite silver-gilt vine leaves might have scrolling tendrils and pierced names, perhaps Sauterne, Chablis, Claret or Madeira. Scallop-shells were popular, as were anchors, goblets, cornucopias and Bacchanalian cherubs. The sought-after kidney shape was made after approximately 1760, while the classically-ornamented goblet shape and the star date generally from the last 25 years or so of the eighteenth century. Just as die-stamping had replaced hand techniques in approximately 1790, so this in its turn was generally superseded by casting in the nineteenth century, and labels lacked the delicate appearance of eighteenth century examples since they became larger and were cast in heavily-ornate designs. The hitherto-vast demand for wine labels virtually ceased after 1860 when a Licensing Act required the labelling of bottles sold by stores and shops. However, electro-plated versions were still produced.

From 1790 all wine labels were subject to hallmarking. They were among the articles specifically mentioned in hallmark amendments of this date which required certain objects to be marked even though they might weigh less than five pennyweights. Whatever their weight they hung on delicate silver chains from the bottle or decanter neck. The hoop or bottle ring label dates from around the last two decades of the century and was shaped so that it would fit neatly around either the neck of a bottle without deep shoulders or certain decanters. A less wide variety of labels was produced concurrently in Sheffield plate, possibly because the fronts of these necessitated a thicker coating of silver if the name was to be engraved, and they were far plainer.

Wine cisterns, wine fountains and wine coolers

Brief mention must be made of these vessels, since they were among the most prestigious pieces of silver made during post-Restoration years. These massive pieces are rare, since most were subsequently melted down owing to the great weight of silver they yielded.

The wine cistern, sometimes weighing as much as 200 or 300 ounces, was shaped like a small bath and was used to hold bottles of wine, keeping them cool on ice. The wine fountain, as its name implies, was used for decanted wine and was an urn-shaped vessel with a cover, usually elaborately decorated with a protruding 'tap' controlled by a spigot, out of which the wine flowed. Wine coolers were intended to hold a single bottle of wine on ice, and were of varying forms, generally based on classical shapes such as the urn or vase, with small handles on either side.

Wine labels, late eighteenth or early nineteenth century.

12 | Boxes

Vinaigrettes

The name of these tiny, shallow boxes often puzzles people since they think of vinegar in terms of its culinary implications. However, in this case it refers to an aromatic acid-based liquid to which these little boxes owe their existence. The introduction of this concentrated aromatic vinegar, which might contain camphor, lavender, cinnamon, bergamot or other pungent-smelling ingredients, meant that a very much smaller type of sponge box could be carried and used on its own as a type of smelling 'bottle', the sponge emitting the concentrated perfume in which it had been soaked. Originally such boxes were described as aromatic vinegar boxes and were simply very small editions of the sponge box, which resembled a snuff box. During the 1780s a change occurred in their basic design, however, and a pierced, hinged inner lid was incorporated, beneath which would be placed the tiny piece of soaked sponge, thus when the outer lid was opened, the aromatic vinegar could be inhaled through the pierced grille or inner lid. Old sponges found in vinaigrettes today may still possess some of their original aroma.

These boxes, which soon became known as vinaigrettes, were exceedingly small at first. Their shapes and dimensions vary, but an oblong one might be about one-and-a-half inches long by just over half-an-inch wide, the depth being just sufficient for the sponge which might be about a quarter-of-an-inch. More common were rectangular versions which might be a little over an inch in width and about one-and-a-half inches long, though some might be even smaller. The piercing of the inner lids at this stage was of a basic, simple form, though the outer lid was more ornate, perhaps engraved or later bright-cut.

Gradually the piercing of the grille became more elaborate, and might be gilded and chased with flowers and leaves, scrolls, fruit and birds. At the same time the overall dimensions of the box increased, so that after a few years, nineteenth century examples were larger, heavier, and lacking the light, fragile quality of their predecessors. They were also far more ornate. They might be chased or engraved with a variety of ornament, perhaps incorporating a cartouche in the centre of the outer lid for the owner's initials. After about 1830 they might incorporate a ring so that they could be worn on a chain (or châtelaine), and from about 1840 the edges of the box might be elaborately shaped.

Vinaigrettes are fascinating objects, and they have long been avidly collected, with a corresponding steep rise in prices. Despite their small size they should be hallmarked, usually on the interior of the base of the box and inside the lid. Some are marked with the sterling lion on the inside of the grille. Most bear the anchor mark of origin since they generally came from Birmingham. Among important Birmingham box-makers were: Samuel Pemberton, Matthew Linwood, Nathaniel Mills, Joseph Taylor, and Joseph Willmore, to mention but a few, and boxes by such makers usually command higher prices.

Apart from vinaigrettes of an oblong, oval, square or hexagonal form, there were those which were made in the shapes of objects, often most realistically, the diversity and ingenuity of which is striking proof of the high degree of craftsmanship of the Birmingham box-makers. They might be formed as tiny purses, books, hearts, shells, policemen's lamps, beehives, walnuts, roses, crowns and tigers' heads. The range seemed limitless, but outstanding among them was the articulated fish, a superb creature whose body was flexible and whose head opened to reveal the sponge container. Genuine examples are costly and rare, but glimpses of them may be caught very occasionally in the windows of leading dealers in antique silver.

Another type which has become greatly sought-after with a corresponding and astounding rise in price is that with an historical building embossed or struck on the lid. These were made from around 1830, many by Nathaniel Mills, and depicted a number of buildings, perhaps including Windsor Castle, St Paul's Cathedral, Warwick Castle or the Crystal Palace. Sometimes the subjects are not so simple to determine as these. By this time ornament was often carried out by mechanical means, which in most cases did not lessen the attraction and, in fact, often added to it. Vinaigrettes were made until well after the middle of the nineteenth century, when they were gradually succeeded by the various forms of smelling bottle.

Snuff boxes

At the beginning of Queen Anne's reign the taking of snuff became popular in England, thought to be as a result of the vast amounts which infiltrated the London market following the capture of Spanish ships carrying snuff in the action of Vigo Bay. It had been introduced to Europe many years before, the Spaniards having first tried it following the discovery by Cortes of Mexicans taking snuff in 1520. The taking of snuff persisted despite two popes issuing bulls against the strange new habit, and, in fact, became exceedingly fashionable during the eighteenth century. It still has a following today.

Victorian shaped vinaigrette, the lid embossed and chased in high relief with a view of the Dublin Exhibition building of 1853, by Nathaniel Mills, Birmingham.

Early Victorian vinaigrette by Nathaniel Mills, Birmingham, 1837, the cover with a chased view of Newstead Abbey.

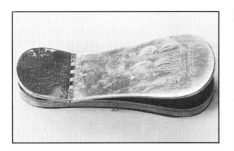

Far left: snuff grater engraved with the crest of Edmonds (Yorkshire) and monogram, *circa* 1700. *Left:* snuff grater formed from a stag cowry-shell mounted in silver, early eighteenth century.

Snuff boxes were made to suit all financial means and came into general use during the earlier years of the eighteenth century, the number produced soon increasing to meet the demand. Those intended to be carried are distinguishable from the tobacco box by a hinged lid, which was necessary in order that one hand could be left free to take the snuff. Larger, hingeless types were made for side-tables in the home. Lids invariably fitted perfectly so that the fine powder would not escape in the pocket. Snuff boxes in Sheffield plate were generally rectangular although other shapes were also produced and tortoiseshell was commonly used for linings, bases and covers. It is not difficult to distinguish between sterling silver and Sheffield plate examples since, quite apart from quality and the fine decoration on silver examples, the Sheffield plate version has usually worn at the edges and corners to reveal the glow of the copper. Those made in precious metals might be plain or decorated, perhaps richly embossed and gilded, and set with precious and semi-precious stones or incorporating enamel miniatures.

Eighteenth century silver examples abound, one of their most attractive characteristics being the beauty of the hinges which might merge into the decorative patterns in such a way as to be sometimes almost indistinguishable. Nineteenth century examples were also decorated variously, but unlike earlier examples also included mechanical ornament. Many of the more pedestrian specimens can show great signs of wear, perhaps being dented or with ill-fitting lids, though high prices may still be asked. Try to avoid anything too dilapidated.

Tobacco boxes

By the last few years of the sixteenth century, tobacco was being smuggled into Cornwall in growing quantities by Flemish, French and Cornish men. The habit of smoking was increasing and the clay pipe was fast becoming an accepted indulgence. Silver tobacco boxes appeared a few decades later, growing in numbers until, by the turn of the eighteenth century, they had become quite numerous. Usually oval in shape with a separate lid, those made during the earlier years of the century were merely functional containers, which were usually undecorated, but might perhaps have a cartouche for a crest or initials. The fashion for oval tobacco boxes began to decline towards the middle of the eighteenth century, although later copies were made.

Top of silver-gilt snuff box, by Rawlings and Summers, 1833.

Snuff box by C. Reily and G. Storer, London, 1839.

Top of snuff box by F. Clark, Birmingham, 1847.

Far left: tobacco box, engraved with the arms of Williamson, Cumberland, late seventeenth century.

Left: cigar box by James Vickery, the lid set with a large panel chased in low relief with a village scene in the manner of Teniers, with plain sides and cedar lining, London, 1892.

Nutmeg graters

A curious little box, the nutmeg grater was in constant use by both men and women throughout the eighteenth century and for many years of the nineteenth. They owed their popularity to our ancestors' addiction to freshly-ground spices in food or drink, particularly punch, mulled ales and wines or hot negus. Simple, early nutmeg graters of the late seventeenth century and beginning of the eighteenth century were usually of a heart shape or 'teardrop' form and, like most of their successors, they were just large enough to hold a nutmeg. In general they had two hinged 'lids', the second of which was what would usually form the base of the box. Beneath the normal lid would be a fitted rasp or grater, and the nutmeg would be kept in a cavity below this. It would be removed via the hinged base, grated on the rasp and the flow of powdered spice allowed to escape through the bottom. Another type, tubular in form, had a separate lid and a removable rasp inside, and other versions also existed. Early examples might be decorated in a primitive way, perhaps with a crudely-engraved flower or the owner's initials.

Silver-gilt spice box, 1690, length two-and-a-half inches.

Many types appeared during the eighteenth century, running concurrently with a simple rectangular box similar to a snuff box. They included acorns, reeded barrels, eggs, urns, maces, walnuts, strawberries, goblets and silver-mounted cowry-shells, to mention but a few. Ornament included engraving and bright-cutting. Nineteenth century examples were increasingly decorated by mechanical means, a popular technique being that of engine-turning, and most of the later examples were rectangular or box-shaped. Very small, lightweight nutmeg graters made during the eighteenth century are commonly found without hallmarks. Nutmeg graters were also produced in Sheffield plate from the 1760s, including heart-shaped boxes, egg-shaped, urn-shaped, circular, oval, rectangular and square. As with silver, the variety of forms was diverse.

Counter boxes

Counter boxes are generally tubular in shape, approximately one-and-a-half inches high and about one inch in diameter, though sometimes less. Lids might be sparingly decorated, perhaps with floral engravings, piercing, or embossed with an impression of the sovereign's bust. The exterior of the circular body was often strengthened by ribbing. The counters, which were decorated in a similar fashion to the lid, were used instead of money in games. They might also, therefore, resemble thinner versions of contemporary coins. Their number varied but it was seldom less than 20. Sides of the boxes were also sometimes pierced.

Above: pierced counter boxes, seventeenth century.

Left: pierced counter boxes and counters, seventeenth century.

Patch boxes

'Han't I got too many beauty spots on? In my mind now, my face looks just like a plumcake' (1706, Mrs Centlivre, *The Platonick Lady*). The lady might well have been right, for patches were applied to the face with considerably more enthusiasm than discretion in many cases, which accounted for some bizarre effects. Stars, crescents, lozenges, half-moons and circular spots were commonplace enough, applied lavishly usually with the aid of mastik, but even more outrageous were the mammoth varieties like a horsedrawn carriage perhaps galloping across the forehead, or a ship in full sail rounding the nose like the Cape of Good Hope. Such items of facial fantasy were of great importance and were carefully kept by the wealthy in small silver patch boxes. These were simple in the beginning, some dating from the seventeenth century, but gradually became more ornate, though never too much so, as the following century progressed.

Patch boxes were mostly circular, ranging in size from tiny examples, measuring approximately threequarters-of-an-inch in diameter and about half-an-inch deep, to around one inch in diameter and about the same depth. Some might be a little larger in diameter. Their pull-off lids might be simply decorated with a small amount of engraving, which sometimes appeared on the sides and around the base of the box too. During the later decades of the eighteenth century certain larger sizes were also introduced including, in about the 1790s, an elliptical example, often superbly bright-cut with floral and foliate motifs and measuring about three-and-a-half inches in length. These were also sometimes of silver-gilt and might well have served other uses, for the fashion for the patch began to dwindle at about this time. Look for hallmarks inside the box on the base or the lid. You may not find a full set, but you should find some. Make sure the lid pulls off easily, as it may be either too tight – usually the case – or too loose. It should fit perfectly; if this is not the case, then the box may have been damaged at some time, a frequent occurrence with such small and fragile objects. Patch box decoration, although sparse, roughly followed contemporary styles of fashion. Early examples were usually hammered up from the flat while later boxes were joined at a seam and soldered. Patch boxes were popular subjects from the early days of Sheffield plate.

Card cases

Typical of the types of ornament which appeared on small nineteenth century boxes is the decoration which embellished card cases, made mostly in Birmingham in great numbers during that century, for the carrying of personal visiting cards. The general measurements of these slender cases were approximately four inches long by three inches wide, and their covers were usually of the hinged slip-over variety. Hallmarks will generally be found on the exterior side of the rim at the top of the body which is concealed when the cover is closed. Decoration included a hand-engraved scene set against a concentric engine-turned background contained within a frame of scroll and foliate pattern, intermingled with more engine-turning and perhaps an architectural motif in each corner; repoussé work in high relief; shaped edges similar to those found on

Shaped card case, engraved on one side with a view of the Scott Memorial, Edinburgh, maker's mark FM, Birmingham, 1868.

contemporary vinaigrettes; and scrolled cartouches in the centre of the case for the owner's initials. Recent years have seen a sharp rise in prices, particularly for the 'castle top' card case, which depicts an important historical building, but others less in demand may still be bought for a reasonable sum. Towards the end of the nineteenth century a plainer style appeared, together with Art Nouveau inspired ornament and one or two revived styles. Card cases were also made in silver-gilt.

Vesta boxes

Vesta boxes are still among the lower-priced nineteenth century collectable objects, despite the fact that the more ornate varieties rise correspondingly in price. These utilitarian little boxes were originally designed to carry vesta matches safely, since when these first appeared they were extremely combustible. Incorporated in the case was a rasp upon which the match was struck. Vesta boxes were made in large quantities from around the middle of the century, and came mostly from Birmingham. Their hallmarks, like those on card cases, should be found on the outside rim of the main case which is concealed by the hinged cover when closed. Sometimes the case incorporated a small ring so that it could be suspended from a watch chain. Although many are quite plain, others may be decorated in elaborate patterns including engine-turned ornament, flat chasing, repoussé work and engraving. Various fanciful shapes were also produced.

Card case, shaped and decorated in high relief on one side with a view of Osborne House, Isle of Wight, and further embossed with foliage. Maker's mark AT, Birmingham, 1854.

Above: late Victorian vesta case in the form of a Brazil nut, 1896.

Left: late Victorian vesta cases, one shaped as a pig and the other as a fish.

Stamp boxes

Also still comparatively inexpensive, stamp boxes have a certain charm because of their Lilliputian size. They are among the numerous nineteenth century objects which at one time were of no importance at all to collectors, but which, with the growing interest in less expensive items, have gradually been included in the list of collectables. Look carefully for these tiny 'envelope' boxes on trays of small items displaying Victorian or early twentieth century jewellery, pieces of silver and so on. They are not easy to spot at a cursory glance because of their postage-stamp size, but are worth considering. They may have a ring fixed to them because they sometimes hung from a châtelaine.

Candlesticks

Although the primitive method of lighting the home by candles has long been outmoded, candle production thrives today for decorative and ornamental reasons. Thus a continuity of this ancient form of lighting is maintained, and with it the need for the traditional candlestick in silver, Sheffield plate or electro-plate. Candlesticks in precious metals were slow to come into the ordinary home, which is hardly surprising since, although the two guilds of tallow-chandlers and wax-chandlers were incorporated in the later years of the fifteenth century, only from the early eighteenth century did candles brighten the house of the more prosperous working man. Before this they would be found in abundance only in the great houses of the land, or for ecclesiastical use the pricket candlestick was adopted since it took the form of a conical spike which would support any type of candle. Variations of these were sometimes made for certain domestic uses, although not usually in silver.

Despite the fact that silver candlesticks are recorded in early inventories, no silver socket examples exist earlier than the seventeenth century, although a candlestick in the royal inventory of 1532 was described as being accompanied by a chain and snuffers, and engraved with H and K, a rose and a pomegranate. After the Restoration in 1660, the socket candlestick – first mentioned in the sixteenth century – was ambitiously produced in fine silver and took its place amidst the profusion of domestic silver upon which fortunes were being spent and invested. Stems were hammered up from the flat and were formed into cylindrical architectural shapes, for architecture was taking on a new significance, which was reflected in the design of the candlestick. Separately-hammered vertical columns were soldered to the main stem, thus forming a columnar shaft inspired by the Doric column which was then becoming fashionable. Standing from about 11 inches in height, with an octagonal or square moulded base, these candlesticks were commonly made in sets of two, four or six, and by the last decade of the seventeenth century might cost around £16 for a pair, including snuffers and stand. Decoration would be mostly vertical fluting and reeding.

During the last decade of the seventeenth century a different technique was employed in the making of candlesticks, when it became general practice to cast them instead of hammering them up from the flat. The stem and socket were thus cast in two sections and soldered at the sides, and the base was likewise separately cast and joined to the main stem.

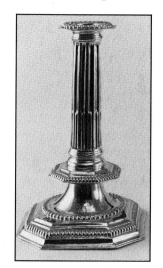

Candlestick, one of a pair, made in London, 1694, the maker's mark TA between the pellets.

Others were cast in one piece. The cast, baluster-shaped candlestick, either plain or with decorative gadrooning around the base and the socket, enjoyed continued popularity for many decades, varying a little over the years to incorporate an octagonal or hexagonal (faceted) stem, and a foot which rose steeply towards the stem instead of being dish-shaped.

More decorative styles appeared during the second decade of the eighteenth century, incorporating naturalistic ornament, masks and shells. The amount of embellishment gradually increased until by 1730 or so the baluster shape had become of secondary importance while overwhelming rococo decoration increased to include such delights as reptiles, birds, fruits, flaming torches, complex scrolls and shell-work. This period produced examples of superlative chased work combined with cast ornamentation. The more decorative candlesticks were sometimes taller – perhaps reaching ten inches – than their plain baluster contemporaries which were still being produced.

During the neo-classical period which followed there were two main outlines for candlesticks: one based on the Corinthian column, complete with capital and base, which was commonly raised upon a classically-decorated, square pedestal, with a socket inside the capital in which a loose nozzle was found; the other had a four-sided pedestal which gradually diminished in size towards its foot. The socket of the latter was commonly in the form of a classical urn and varied decorative effects were based on contemporary motifs. Bases might be round, square or triangular. A circular, tapering stem also became popular with a circular

Baluster candlestick by David Green, London, 1720.

Far left: baluster candlestick decorated with leaf and rope ornament, London, 1759.

Left: neo-classical candlestick, Sheffield, 1776.

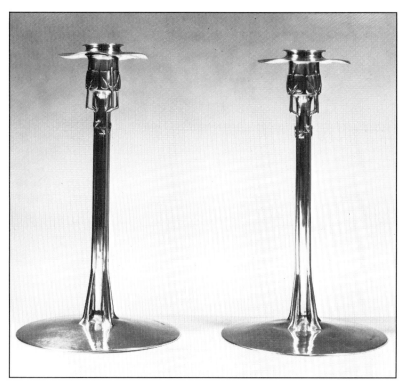

base. These two main shapes have probably been among the most widely-copied of all candlestick styles, and to this day can be bought in new sterling silver or electro-plate. Regency candlesticks which followed once again reverted to rococo styles, while Victorian examples covered a wide spectrum of forms and decorative effects. With the prolific output of Sheffield plate and the introduction of thin silver during the 1770s, candlesticks generally became increasingly more opulent and far less expensive and were made in large sets. Hallmarks on mass-produced examples of candlesticks are generally found on the edge of the base, while earlier examples were usually marked beneath the base.

Above left: pair of candlesticks designed by RC for Liberty and Company, Birmingham, 1906.

Above right: one of a pair of candelabra, maker's mark JA, London, 1819.

Candelabra

Candelabra could be easily adapted from suitable candlesticks by the addition of branches, and because of this it is not uncommon to find that the branches are often of a later date than the main stem. Decorative candelabra were popular from the eighteenth century onwards, but it is rare to find them hallmarked before the 1730s. They followed in general the ornament of the ordinary candlesticks, and usually consisted of twin branches which twisted around a central removable finial that concealed a further candle-socket. Candelabra with three branches were also produced. The fashion for candelabra stems and branches reached such heights as the eighteenth century progressed, particularly from the 1760s onwards, that their production became one of the most lucrative sections of the silversmith's work. With the increase in mechanisation and the resultant cutting of costs and general speeding up of production, candelabra were brought within the reach of a growing number of buyers although the quality and standard of workmanship diminished correspondingly. At the same time, however, hand-worked specimens were also available for those who were willing to pay more to obtain better quality.

Chambersticks

Modest and practical, the silver chamberstick was in use during the seventeenth century, but examples are not generally found before the last quarter of the century. In the line of the old nursery rhyme, 'Here comes a candle to light you to bed', the words refer to a chamberstick which consisted of a saucer-shaped base for safety, with a short candle-socket in its centre, and a simple handle by which to carry it around the house. Larger homes might later have an assortment of such chambersticks set upon a table in the hall, a person taking one when it was needed and lighting it from a special master taper. Usually made of a lighter metal, the diameter of the saucer-shaped dish varied but generally measured about six inches, the short socket standing about three inches high. Most late seventeenth and eighteenth century examples would have a shapely scroll handle soldered beneath the base and curving upwards.

The second decade or so of the eighteenth century saw the introduction of the chamberstick which incorporated a pair of snuffers, a slot to contain these being in the dish beneath the candle-socket, at the middle of the round or oblong dish. A cone-shaped extinguisher, perhaps surmounted by a ball finial at the apex, was also commonly included. The socket with a detachable nozzle and wider rim for catching the drips of grease

Chamber candlestick in silver-gilt by Paul de Lamerie, London, 1748.

appeared more generally a few years later. Chambersticks followed contemporary styles in ornament, their rims and bases commonly reeded, and, during the neo-classical period, an urn-shaped candle-socket appeared which was placed on a rectangular tray, often standing upon four ball feet, and decorated by reeding, beading or gadrooning. During the Regency period the dish increased in size and was heavily decorated with naturalistic and shell ornament, as were the snuffers which were similarly chased in high relief.

Until the first decade or so of the nineteenth century chambersticks were available in pairs and sets of varying numbers. Victorian chambersticks generally reverted to the circular dish. One pattern of particularly popular appeal which was produced during the middle of the nineteenth century was in the shape of a leaf with the stalk trailing round to form a handle, and its socket flower-shaped: convolvulus, regina lily and nasturtium being much favoured. Chambersticks were not only useful in years gone by: today they can come into their own during power cuts, and meanwhile they make attractive ornaments.

Below left: pair of George III chamber candlesticks by Samuel Hennell and John Terry, 1814.

Below right: early Victorian miniature chamber candlestick of naturalistic design in the form of waterlilies, by E. E. J. and W. Barnard, 1839.

Snuffers

Candlelight was not at all the romantic vision we tend to have of it today, for there were certain unpleasant side-issues. One was the unctuous aroma which the tallow emitted, particularly when the wick was incorrectly extinguished, and another was that, to provide a steady light, the wick needed to be constantly trimmed since the tallow or wax melted faster than the wick burned. It was not until approximately the time of Queen Victoria that the non-guttering candlestick was introduced which meant that the wick, then made from a more closely-woven structure, eliminated the problem. Previously the greasy wick, if permitted to go unsnuffed, would loll over into the melted fat, resulting in unpleasant fumes and spluttering. A pair of snuffers, therefore, were the answer. Snuffers were a very basic device, in appearance rather like scissors, except that a box was soldered to one blade to contain the charred bits of wick (snuff) cut off by the scissors.

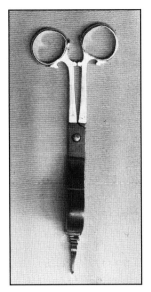

Snuffers of the eighteenth and early nineteenth centuries.

Although snuffers were known before the seventeenth century, it was not until after about 1660 that silver examples began to be mentioned more regularly in inventories and diaries. Samuel Pepys referred in 1667 to a new acquisition: 'this night comes home my new silver snuff dish which I do give myself for my closet', and an item in the papers of Robert Harley, Earl of Oxford, reveals that he paid £3 13s 4d (about £3·67) for snuffers and pan in 1721. Snuffers were generally plain, although the box might be decorated by a little engraving and, in some cases, fluting. The box was perhaps rectangular, oval, semi-circular, lozenge- or barrel-shaped. After approximately the middle of the eighteenth century three feet appeared on the base of snuffers, below the box and two handles. Snuffer handles became increasingly more ornate, and a coiled spring, concealed by a boss, was incorporated at the pivoting joint so that they would remain closed after use. A later development, which lowered the price of snuffers, used steel for the cutting blades and box, while the handles were made in sterling silver. The box, too, might have applied silver decoration. Matthew Boulton and others produced many such separate pieces for snuffers well into the nineteenth century, and the various sections were then joined by silversmiths.

While the utilitarian snuffers did the work, it was the snuffer tray which was the beautiful complement to the prosaic device. It had not always been so. The snuffer tray or dish had played an unimportant role throughout the fashion for the upright snuffer stand incorporating a vertical socket for the snuffer box. This stand had originated in the seventeenth century, and was popular for the first three decades or so of the eighteenth century. But at about this time, with the tide of rococo decoration sweeping through domestic silver, the snuffer tray came into its own as a thing of more beauty than the upright stand which did not lend itself so well to decoration. A gracious scroll handle now adorned the tray, the sides of which curved elegantly inwards, while the everted rims were enhanced with finely-chased rococo motifs. Three ornamental feet were added, and rims became all-important, reflecting the styles of contemporary table-trays. Others might have pierced vertical rims or be elliptical in form until, by the last two decades of the eighteenth century and into the nineteenth, there was an increasingly wide range of styles. Snuffers, too, were generally more elaborate. Trays made after about 1825 were excessively decorated in the usual revived styles. In addition to the wide variety of snuffer dishes in silver, there was an amazing diversity in Sheffield plate, while others were made in Sheffield plate but had decorative sterling silver mounts. Electro-plated examples were also produced.

Tapersticks

Throughout the eighteenth century miniature candlesticks were made, which echoed the fashionable styles of ordinary candlesticks. They usually measured around four to six inches in height and were used to hold slender wax tapers which provided an instant flame before automatic lighting and friction matches came into general use. They were known variously as tobacco candlesticks (for smokers), tapersticks or tea candlesticks. The latter, usually more decorative after about the fourth decade of the eighteenth century, generally held tapers of English beeswax which emitted a more fragrant aroma than other types and was thus better suited to the genteel eighteenth century tea ritual. Chamber tapersticks with small sockets and conical extinguishers, decorated by shell and foliage rims and handles, became more general in the early nineteenth century, particularly in Sheffield plate.

Wax jacks and bougie boxes

Apart from the small flame which tapersticks provided for various domestic purposes, there were also certain gadgets which provided flames for specific requirements, among them 'sealing tapers'. The wax jack and the bougie box are included in this category. The former, found less frequently in sterling silver than in Sheffield plate, is a strange-looking device, consisting of a small saucer-shaped dish with a handle, upon which was set a framework to hold, either vertically or horizontally, a reel of taper which was then inserted through a nozzle. The taper was thus held in an upright position while its flame was utilised. A conical-shaped extinguisher was sometimes attached by a chain, with a tiny stand upon the dish to hold it.

The silver bougie box, also made in Sheffield plate, consisted of a circular 'box' approximately three inches in diameter, with a handle attached, and a hingeless lid, in the centre of which was a funnel-shaped hole with a nozzle through which the taper was taken. No doubt this small box proved especially useful in preventing mice from nibbling the taper. The name bougie derives from Bougiah, the name of the Algerian town from which bleached wax was imported.

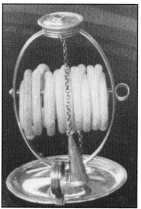

Top: taperstick, London, 1718.

Above: late eighteenth century wax jack by Chawner and Emes.

Toilet sets

Magnificent toilet sets in silver or silver-gilt were typical of the presents which Charles II would give to his more exalted mistresses. According to Samuel Pepys, Lady Byron persuaded Charles to have some £4,000 of silver goods made for her, but she died before these could be given to her. Others revelled in their greed and the Duchess of Cleveland had in her home silver tables, stands, fire irons, sconces and all manner of domestic pieces amounting to a vast fortune. Such splendour was characteristic of the period and certain toilet sets are still in existence as tangible proof of it. The Victoria and Albert Museum, London, has the famous Calverley set, dated 1683, with 13 pieces, but this number is comparatively modest, some sets having around 30 pieces, containing a variety of accessories. However, they nearly all included a mirror in a superb frame, and many boasted bowls with covers as well as basins with accompanying water ewers and candlesticks.

The contents are interesting since they reflect the social habits of the various times in which they were made. They might include little patch boxes when patches were a vital adjunct to contemporary beauty, pomade pots, table bells, pin cushions, small glass jars with silver covers, snuffers and comb boxes. The Ashmolean Museum, Oxford, has one of the finest and most complete examples in existence, made in 1724 by the Huguenot silversmith Paul de Lamerie for George Treby MP, as a wedding present for his wife. Exquisitely made and chased, it was given particularly

Below left: superb William III silver-gilt toilet set by Phillip Rollos, London, *circa* 1695.

Below right: Victorian travelling dressing case with silver-gilt items including 12 mounted bottles or boxes, a spirit burner with screw-on lid, a covered beaker, a tea spoon, pairs of steel scissors with silver-gilt handles, a propelling pencil, needle case and shoe horn. Made for Princess Helena Augusta Victoria (1846-1923), the third daughter of Queen Victoria.

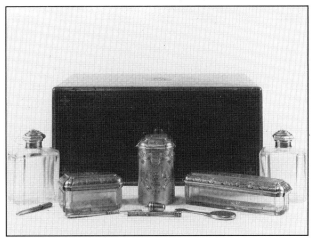

lavish treatment, for which an additional five shillings (25p) an ounce was charged. Many toilet sets later were disbanded and also were melted down when their owners, often ladies of transient fortune, needed the money. When nineteenth and early twentieth century toilet sets have been disbanded, however, the result can be advantageous to collectors of lesser means because one often finds nice little glass jars with hallmarked silver lids, small caskets and the like, which are well worth the collector's attention. Separated items from eighteenth century sets may also be found, but these will be correspondingly higher in price.

Silver-backed brushes

Nineteenth and twentieth century silver-backed hairbrushes, made *en suite* with hand mirrors, can be regarded as a modern progression of the toilet set, from whence the idea originated. Dressing-tables and fitments today could no longer accommodate the array of contents described above, but the silver-backed brush and hand mirror are a different matter. Room might even be found for a pair of scent flasks and a clothes brush: typical contents of a small nineteenth or twentieth century set. Silver-backed brushes of this type might be engraved, engine-turned or embossed with a heavy naturalistic pattern. They should certainly be hallmarked. At one time early twentieth century examples could be had for a song, but this is no longer so. However, they may still be found in provincial shops and often come up for auction.

Bedroom silver and domestic items in an advertisement of 1900.

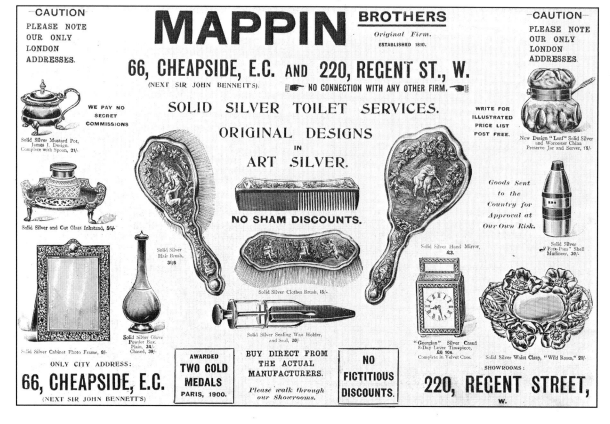

Silver frames for mirrors or photographs

The decorative silver frame, used mostly nowadays for photographs, appeared for mirrors after the Restoration, late seventeenth century oblong examples being heavily ornamented with naturalistic decoration between gadrooning or complex beading, and surmounted by a coat-of-arms in a complex setting. Such fine examples might be among gifts to the royal family or court. Other types of decorative frames were also popular in the eighteenth century, perhaps being made of wood or gesso which was gilded and carved. Nineteenth century silver examples became more numerous not only for mirrors but, in later years and into the Edwardian era, for photographs. Others were extremely rich and ornate, decorated according to the style of the day. A splendid example of this lavish decoration can be seen in the boudoir mirror made in 1862 by L. Morel Ladeuil, who, although trained on the Continent, worked for Elkingtons for many years. Ornament on this gilt mirror includes cherubs holding drapery, and branches entwined with butterflies and flowers. A flamboyant peacock surmounts the top. Although the framework was of gilt decorated with jewels, this elaborate attitude tended to influence silver decoration of the period as well.

In the 1870s a mirror by Wilms, who also worked for Elkingtons, maintained this taste for opulence. One of his oval mirror frames at this time consisted of silver inlaid with gold, the outer frame being of silver decorated with repoussé arabesque and the inner one of steel, bronzed to a deep shade and damascened in silver and gold. Running concurrently with such embellishment were those frames influenced by, among other styles, the classical revival and naturalistic forms, still a favourite for certain types of objects. Late Victorian and Edwardian silver frames varied in size considerably. Watch out for the general condition of these because some have become badly dented over the years, and this does not always reveal itself at a quick glance in examples which are covered with over-all embossing and chasing. Attractive are the frames which were decoratively-shaped or showing the influence of the Art Nouveau movement.

Scent flasks and bottles

Containers for scent would also be incorporated in toilet sets for the fairer sex, and such separated examples exist. Most of those seen today, however, would be nineteenth century, or perhaps late eighteenth century. Nineteenth century silver flasks for perfume can be most decorative but also most expensive. Many of these are very ornate, perhaps with surface engraving in scroll and foliate or floral patterns, heart-shaped or in other decorative forms. They might have a small silver chain fitted to them so that they could be hung by this to a châtelaine. Delightful bottles in plain or coloured glass with plain or decorated silver mounts were made in vast quantities during the nineteenth century and were very attractive, their diversity of shape adding to their interest. Small examples were made for the handbag, and larger ones for the dressing-table. Certain specimens, which look like perfume bottles, incorporate a pierced grille in the lid and may be

Victorian easel-backed mirror with embossed and pierced silver frame by William Comyns, 1900.

Below: Edwardian scent flask modelled as an owl's head set with glass eyes, realistically chased with feathers, by Sampson Mordan and Co, 1902. *Bottom:* cone-shaped scent bottle, the screw top modelled as an owl's head with glass eyes, by Sampson Mordan and Co, 1894.

described as a vinaigrette, scent bottle or smelling bottle. Some silver flasks have a small section at the side which opens for the containment of pills or anything similar.

Shaving basins and accessories

The shaving dish in sterling silver was shaped like its ceramic counterpart, ie it was circular with a large 'bite' out of it to fit around the neck. These were generally undecorated and even those intended for royal stubble usually had only the royal arms and cipher. Silver shaving brushes were also used, and the shaving equipment would be completed by a spherical silver box with hinged lid for the soap. Spherical soap boxes were also made in Sheffield plate from approximately 1770. In either metal they stood upon a circular foot with a stem, the cover of the box – hinged across the centre – either plain or perforated so that the perfume from the soap might pervade the room. Soap boxes intended primarily for shaving kits were generally left unperforated. Measurements were approximately five inches high by about three-and-a-half inches in diameter. Both silver and Sheffield plate examples were similarly decorated, the deep lid being attractively pierced and the mounts of the rim and foot chased with naturalistic motifs including roses, acorns, thistles and so on. The spherical soap box gradually became unfashionable and there was little demand for it after about the 1820s.

Above left: Victorian barrel-shaped vinaigrette-cum-scent bottle, fitted with a chained screw-on stopper, hinged vinaigrette cover and pill compartment, Sampson Mordan and Co, 1871.

Above right: shagreen case of razors with silver mounts, the razors with handles of tortoiseshell also mounted in silver, dating from the first half of the eighteenth century.

Toothpicks, toothpick cases, toothbrushes and toothbrush cases

Silver toothpicks were known in Tudor times and, although they were certainly used during the seventeenth and eighteenth centuries, few survive. Many were appropriately shaped for teeth at one end and rounded or 'cupped' at the other for ears. Toothpick cases, however, are less difficult to find. These are mostly late eighteenth century and attractive, perhaps oval or oblong with cut corners and a lid set on the top of the box, the hinge incorporated into the surface decoration of the lid, with, perhaps, a velvet lining inside. Decoration included engraving and bright-cutting, and filigree examples were also made.

A primitive form of toothbrush was in use at least as early as the seventeenth century, but a less crude example eventually emerged towards the end of the following century. This had a silver handle and a rectangular frame into which the brush component could be fitted and removed for cleansing or replacement. Silver toothbrush boxes were made to contain these and might be plain or decorated with neo-classical motifs. There was also a tooth etui produced at about this time which contained the toothbrush – with removable brush portion – double-ended silver tongue scraper and toothpowder box. Some toothbrushes incorporated a small compartment with a hinged lid, for toothpowder, at the end of their handle, the toothbrush also having a neat silver box in which it could be kept. Other examples of toothbrushes featured slender circular silver handles coming from the brush end to which would be joined a circular green ivory handle. But despite these attractive dental aids, the cleaning of teeth was generally practised only intermittently. Perhaps one can understand why when one discovers that a usual recipe for toothpowder at that time would probably contain cuttlefish bone, areca nut or pumice stone.

Unusual silver-mounted glass macassar-oil spray, the body moulded as a cuirass and fitted with a silver cover in the form of a knight's visage with a funnel fitted to his lips. Maker's mark TS, London, 1882.

Inkstands

Inkstands (standishes) were much favoured in both sterling silver and, from about 1760, Sheffield plate. Silver examples include the treasury inkstand: a rectangular box which contained an inkpot, pounce box and wafer box – a small adhesive disk for sealing letters – with a single- or double-hinged lid and perhaps a drawer below for quills. Another type, made in both silver and Sheffield plate, consisted of a rectangular tray, standing upon four small feet, which had three sockets. In the case of the silver version, the inkpot and pounce box would fit into the outer two sockets, while the middle one would contain a small hand bell, or taperstick for sealing. The pens would either be placed in a trough at the front of the tray or stood in holes around the top of the inkpot. The Sheffield plate version would contain three flint-glass pots for ink, pounce and shot. This tray type provided the basic form for subsequent inkstands, and continued to be made until the later years of the eighteenth century when the word inkstand replaced that of standish, and when flint-glass containers also appeared on silver trays. The design was maintained throughout the nineteenth century.

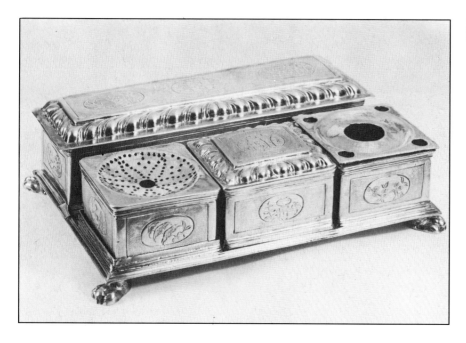

Inkstand by Anthony Nelme, London, *circa* 1685.

An unusual shape was the 'globe' inkstand, also made in sterling silver and Sheffield plate, which was formed as a spherical container standing on either four elegantly-scrolled feet, or one circular foot. John Robins of Clerkenwell Green, London, produced the silver examples which appeared towards the end of the 1780s and which were soon being copied in Sheffield plate. The globe had a hollow body divided into two separate parts, the whole being contained within a framework. The hollow globe was opened by pressing a spring-loaded terminal, and contained various items of writing equipment including two or three glass bottles – sometimes in Bristol blue glass cut square with chamfered shoulders – penknife, pencil and ivory writing tablets. The globe might be decorated with swags of foliate motifs and lion's head masks, or other classical ornament. The usual size was around nine-and-a-half inches in height and five inches in diameter, but giant examples up to 12 inches in height and nearly six inches in diameter were also made.

Georgian and the better nineteenth century inkstands command high prices, but it is still possible to find individual pieces from disbanded inkstands. Perforated pounce dredgers, for example, are an interesting reminder of the necessity to sprinkle absorbent writing paper with pounce (the powder of gum sandarach) so that the ink would not 'run'. When glazed paper was introduced in the nineteenth century the ink was dried by sprinkling fine sand over it. There might also be a container for lead shot which was used to remove from the quill the imperfections accumulated in the thick, crude ink. When glass containers came into fashion, the quill cleaner, too, would be of glass, and the rim of the cover would be pierced with holes in which the quills were inserted. Sometimes the quill cleaner and ink were in the same container, the ink being kept within a glass liner and the lead shot in an exterior cavity.

Below left: inkstand by Paul de Lamerie, London, 1729.

Below right: globe inkstand, late eighteenth century.

Inkstand by Joseph and John Angell, London, 1841.

Sheffield plate inkstands were made in a vast number of designs, and the shapes of their glass containers, like those in silver examples, included either plain or diamond-cut shoulders. A square-shaped container also became popular, which was fluted to the shoulders and decorated with the fashionable diamond-cutting. After George IV ascended the throne, the shapes of containers included urn, vase, melon and circular forms. Covers were generally loose until about 1815, from which time they were given hinges.

Shapes of late eighteenth century inkstand trays included a rectangular form with pierced sides and matching container sockets. There was as well a canoe-shaped tray with pierced sides, and sometimes with swing handles. It was a particularly fashionable example and its popularity continued well into the Victorian era. Cheaply-produced machine-made inkstands of the late eighteenth and nineteenth centuries which chiefly emanated from Birmingham and Sheffield were made concurrently with beautifully-produced and decorated examples made by master craftsmen. Whatever category inkstands fell into, the range and variety was enormous, amounting to hundreds over the years, the diversity of which increased as the nineteenth century progressed when even more shapes and types of ornament appeared in the miscellany of designs. Collectors looking for cut-glass inkstand containers with sterling silver mounts should remember that these will nearly always be hallmarked, since, although small, they were not exempt from hallmarking.

The little hand bells incorporated in eighteenth century standishes are among the separated items which occasionally become available. They are smaller than general table bells and much sought-after, with the result that these sweet-sounding bells are costly. They have been much-copied over the years.

Propelling pencils and novelty pens

The interest in writing implements as collectable items has increased greatly over recent years, and now the sort of articles which at one time would not even have commanded a second glance have become established in their own right. Among the general pieces dating from the late eighteenth century are such objects as paper knives, quill pen cutters, pen holders and propelling pencils. The latter two in particular fall into the province of sterling silver, and nineteenth or early twentieth century propelling pencils offer scope for beginners. These were made in a variety of forms and were decorated, plain or in the form of novelties. They are not always hallmarked and tests should be made to ensure in

Left: novelty inkstand in the form of fruit, by Robert Hennell, London, 1845.

Above: novelty inkstand with taperstick in the form of an agile circus performer with one leg upon a rustic ladder. The inkwell is formed as a drum, and the pen holder as a basket of victuals with an upturned top hat. Elkington and Company, 1853.

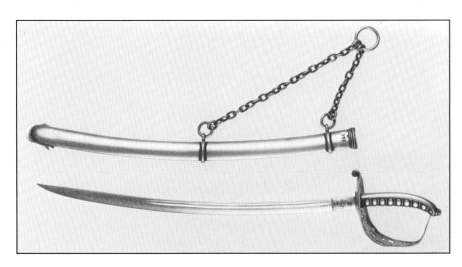

Paper knife in the form of a dress sword and sheath, maker's mark JB, London, 1874.

doubtful cases that they are of silver. Some tend to be shoddy, but others are substantial and well-made. Sterling silver cases which fitted over a blacklead pencil like a sheath – sometimes oblong with an oblong pencil – are generally undecorated with a slip-on cover which goes over the lead. Decorated examples, when found, are most attractive.

Ink erasers, sometimes with a die-stamped silver handle and steel blade for eradicating blots by judicious scratching, may also be added to the list of recently-popular collectables, as well as certain types of penknives, including early twentieth century examples which have now risen in price. These are the sort of pieces which are appropriate for beginners, since a collection of writing paraphernalia as a whole need not be limited to sterling silver objects only and thus the general cost can be lessened. Reputable London auction houses already consider this sort of writing equipment of sufficiently high value to hold periodical sales of this once-valueless equipage.

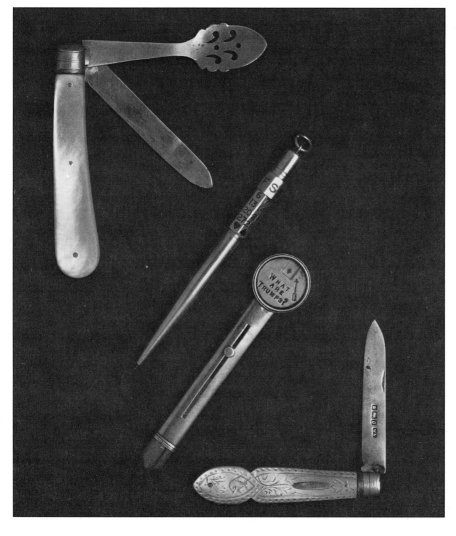

Top to bottom: orange peeler and fruit knife, Birmingham, 1903; calendar pencil, Birmingham, 1937; Bridge pencil, Birmingham, 1904; and penknife, Birmingham, 1893.

Tazzas, salvers, waiters and trays

Late nineteenth century electro-plated waiters cost around a quarter of the price of their sterling silver counterparts and were practically indistinguishable from them at first glance. This also applied to large tea trays with moulded handles which were handsomely decorated with rococo-style rim patterns and surface ornament. It is hardly surprising, then, that electro-plated trays appeared so numerously in homes everywhere. They were a direct descendant of the tazza, a fashionable seventeenth century piece with an approximate diameter of 12 inches, which declined in popularity after about 1715-20. These small trays, usually with a central depression and often of heavy silver, stood upon a central foot. They might be decorated with embossing and chasing or engraving, or with a crest in the centre, gadrooning around the foot and edge of the rim being very usual. Sometimes they were plain. They were gradually superseded by the waiter, which had three or four moulded decorative feet instead of the single stem, and which might be used by servants to proffer small objects, usually being made in sets of varying numbers. The larger salver was similarly employed.

Below left: waiter with the mark of John Tuite, London, 1721.

Below right: waiter by Richard Rugg, London, 1771.

Waiter by Richard Rugg,
London, 1777.

The rims of eighteenth century waiters and salvers are of particular importance because these were of great decorative appeal, sometimes consisting of up to ten ornate curved sections. Square or rectangular examples during the 1720s would have decoratively-shaped rounded corners. Circular salvers became popular from the 1730s and featured beautiful, moulded pie-crust rims consisting of several sections which were decorated with rococo shells and gadrooning, resembling the pie-crust borders on tripod tables, although the salvers generally preceded the tables. Others were variously shaped. Until the middle of the century these separately-moulded borders were produced concurrently with hand-raised rims in decoratively-shaped outlines which might also be enriched with applied borders consisting of small, ornate castings of rococo motifs such as shells, scrolls, masks and vine leaves. Hand-raised decoration would be enriched by piercing and embossing. The period is notable for this fine work which continued until the neo-classical influence made itself felt. By the 1760s a less positive type of decoration had appeared, sometimes with gadrooning on the rims and with inner borders of classical motifs including swags and wheat-ears. The extravagant rims of the rococo period then disappeared until the revival of this style early in the nineteenth century, but the original perfection was never again achieved.

The silver tea tray was an important part of tea equipage. It was of an adequate size to hold the numerous items required for the infusion of tea and might be anything up to around two feet in diameter, raised upon four decorative feet and similar to smaller versions, being likewise mass-produced towards the later years of the eighteenth century. An

Tray embossed with decoration of peacocks, designed by Charles Ashbee, London, 1896.

elliptical shape became popular at this time and rims included those which were applied and strengthened with beading. Others were ornately pierced and often decorated with classical motifs. Hand grips also became general.

By the time George IV ascended the throne the rectangular tray was in fashion, usually adorned with a generous amount of chasing. Victorian examples, made in sterling silver, Sheffield plate and electro-plate, were lavishly decorated with an agglomeration of ornament. The work of the nineteenth century designer and sculptor, Alfred Stevens, who produced designs for both silver and electro-plate, can be typified by his tray with a rim of scrolls, acanthus leaves and rams' heads, which incorporated an ovolo border. Within this enthusiastically-applied decoration were more visual feasts in the form of richly-engraved strapwork and stylised foliage. An electro-plated version, made by Thomas Bradbury and Sons of Sheffield in 1856, is in the possession of the Victoria and Albert Museum, London.

Buckles

Buckles were a functional form of personal ornament which brought delight to fashionable men and women throughout practically the entire eighteenth century. Their size varied according to the dictates of fashion. 'The Beaus wore their buckles so very large that they were obliged to buckle them to the shoe with a false strap', records John Crosier in his diary for 1787. In the *Ipswich Journal* for the same year a correspondent points out that 'she used to fasten her shoe with a circle scarcely larger than a bird's eye, and since, she has fastened it with a parallelogram as large as the buckle of a coach-spring'. However, buckles generally were oblong or square and modestly proportioned between approximately 1700 and about 1725, and it was only after this that they began to increase in size. They reached vast dimensions by the 1770s when the Artois buckle was introduced, which was worn by both men and women. It was named after the Comte d'Artois and, according to current publications, the young fops about town wore these with such pride that they scarcely noticed how heavy they were, although the silver sometimes weighed as much as eight or ten ounces.

In addition to silver, Sheffield plate and gold, buckles were also made of white metal, steel and pinchbeck, perhaps set with Bristol stones, paste jewels or diamonds. They not only appeared on shoes but also on other parts of the attire including men's kneebands and hats and women's girdles and neck-bands. A wealthy man might be the lucky owner of as many as a couple of dozen buckles, some of which would be silver; suitably decorated for town wear or plainer for pastoral activities. By the final years of the eighteenth century they had become so important that it was rumoured the Prince of Wales had such a variety he could choose a different one for every day of the year.

Silver-gilt cloak buckle by Paul Storr, London, 1830.

Eighteenth century buckles were decorated in a wide assortment of ways, those made during the rococo period bearing a profusion of shells, scrolls, and other types of ornament, while later examples were engraved or bright-cut. Some were also gilded. Many were perfectly plain, and it is to this less-ostentatious variety that an affluent tradesman might aspire for use on Sundays or other special occasions. By the later years of the eighteenth century the buckle-making trade employed a vast army of workers in the Midlands, but, alas, by the end of the century, buckles had finally declined in fashion. A certain number continued to be made during the nineteenth century, particularly during the later years when they sometimes came under the influence of Art Nouveau.

Buttons

Buttons were made in various metals including gold, silver, gilt, Sheffield plate (see chapter 5), pewter, steel, wire and brass. With the exception of certain metal buttons, they were generally dome-shaped during the first half of the eighteenth century and usually of a medium or small size. Until the days of Elizabeth I, buttons had been ornamental only, since clothes were fastened by aiglets or hooks-and-eyes and various other devices. Nevertheless, buttons were popular even then, as can be seen in contemporary portraits whose subjects are often dressed in costumes liberally decorated by this form of ornament. Very early silver buttons, however, have mostly disappeared over the years.

It was not until the eighteenth century that they were really documented for they are mentioned in various contemporary publications which reveal some interesting, if curious, occurrences. For example, legislation early in the eighteenth century declared it illegal to wear covered buttons, yet it would appear from the surviving examples of men's coats and waistcoats that this was not taken very seriously, since they commonly have buttons covered in the same fabric as the garment. On the other hand, the law was enforced from time to time, as in the case of the following incident reported in the *Ipswich Journal*. A gentleman had unthinkingly strolled into the Guildhall Court of Justice, London, to see if anything of interest was afoot. It was noted that he was wearing covered buttons and he was immediately fined for this offence at the rate of £2 a dozen. This may not seem much by comparison with the number of buttons upon a man's outfit today, but in the eighteenth century they were used numerously, perhaps forming two parallel rows on the waistcoat, with a line stretching from the neck almost to the hem of the frockcoat, and still more on the sleeves and cuffs. The legislation against covered buttons was happily later repealed.

Silver buttons survive in sets of six, eight or more which is not surprising since it was usual for a gentleman's buttons to match throughout his attire. They were also made *en suite* with link buttons. Hallmarking is rare on earlier eighteenth century examples, but may sometimes appear on the face of the button, an unsightly practice. After 1790 hallmarked examples became more common because, despite their small size and weight, they were no longer exempt from that time. They were made in all sorts of patterns and designs, including a vast selection of scenes, sporting motifs, crests, and so on. After the second half of the century buttons were usually flattish and not so highly domed and after approximately the 1770s they became larger. Huge buttons became fashionable at about this time and remained popular into the 1780s.

Silver and gold buttons were usually worn only by gentlemen, and a person might be judged by the condition and style of his buttons, the less-affluent wearing a mixed and worn selection. A snooty description in *A Trip Through the Town,* published in 1735, describes 'a pretty corpulent man whose plate-buttons coat denoted him the master of some publick house'. Plated buttons later became accepted when the dazzling new Sheffield plate was introduced, and thousands were made in this respectable plated copper (see chapter 5). Silver buttons are costly but

Top to bottom: button with decorative border, *circa* 1899; Elizabeth I coin made into a button; button with Celtic design, *circa* 1900; Art Nouveau button, 1904; castle button, 1910.

take heart from the case of the collector who, when browsing, came across a black metal button which he bought for £3. After cleaning it with care, late Georgian hallmarks appeared on what revealed itself to be a superb silver button.

Button hooks

This natural adjunct to the button may not be a very glamorous object, but at the time of writing it does still have one advantage over many other items – it is usually reasonably priced in less-fashionable haunts. The button hook came into its own from around the middle of the nineteenth century to the 1920s, although it was used before this time. Button hooks were made in large numbers to help the army of desperate ladies with the fiddling and trying task of fastening tight buttons on gloves, footwear and the varying types of uncompromising stiffer fabrics which were then so fashionable. Handles of button hooks were commonly of silver, although there were other types, often heavily-embossed in rococo swirls and floral or foliate designs. The shaft was of steel, which was hooked at the end for dealing with the recalcitrant buttons, and some have more than one hook for varying sizes of buttons. Silver handles should be hallmarked but will not bear Queen Victoria's bust (the duty mark) after 1890. On some the marks have become rather worn.

Needlework accessories

Considering the amount of time women spent plying their needle, the group of silver items including thimbles, thimble buckets, pin cushions, bodkins and needle cases, is not extensive, particularly with earlier items. The position improves much later, during the Victorian era and into the twentieth century, so in order to avoid frustration it is well worth considering the later examples when starting or adding to a collection.

Thimble, *circa* 1750-1820.

Among these are silver *thimbles* which can make a stunning collection when grouped together for display. Silver thimbles were used in the sixteenth and seventeenth centuries, but those which are usually available are not of this type, and even eighteenth century specimens have become far less easy to find. Nineteenth century thimbles were variously decorated, sometimes depicting topical subjects, or mottoes such as 'God Save the Queen'. Ordinary examples are still quite reasonably priced and the range of designs and borders varies. Henry Griffith and Company, a gold and silversmith firm in Birmingham, produced vast numbers of silver thimbles in an enormous variety from 1856 until as recently as 1956. However, silver thimbles should be examined carefully before they are bought – there is a variance in the quality as well as the design.

Thimble buckets were used to contain the thimble when it was suspended from a châtelaine. The little bucket, often nicely decorated, would have two rings for the small silver chain.

A rare but delightful item is the silver *bodkin,* mentioned in records as early as the fifteenth century, which was an aid to threading ribbon or tape. Early examples might be around five-and-a-half inches long, with a large threading eye and simple, crude decorative engraving. An ornamental loop or similar shape appeared just above the eye and this was topped by a 'cupped' or rounded piece of silver, which might have been used for cleaning the ears. Sometimes the owner's initials might be engraved roughly or pricked out, while the maker's mark appears on others. They seldom date later than the seventeenth century.

Pin cushions can be charming, mostly because of their varying shapes which include circular, heart, a rare book type with domed covers, piglets, owls, fluffy chicks, boots and so on. The padded portion is contained within the silver frame. Less ingenious silver mounts may be plain, or lightly decorated, sometimes with an ornamental edge which looks very pretty against the cushion. Early pin cushions might be stuffed with emery powder or similar abrasive, so that the pins would stay clean while they were in the cushion. Until about 100 years ago, the steel which was used to make pins and needles tended to rust quickly under usual atmospheric conditions.

Bodkin/needle cases, although they do exist, may take some time to find, particularly Georgian examples. Early nineteenth century specimens are very attractive, usually being engraved or bright-cut, but these are sadly often in dubious condition. They may have hinged (rare) or slip-off lids, the hinges sometimes being incorporated on the top of the lid and integrated into the design of the lid pattern. Those with slip-off lids vary in length and take the form of narrow, tapering, flat 'tubes'.

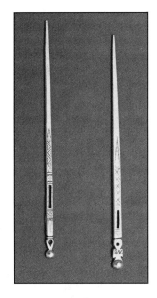

Above: two Elizabeth I bodkins, *circa* 1595.

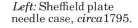

Left: Sheffield plate needle case, *circa*1795.

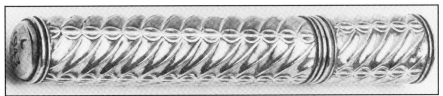

The *châtelaine,* when hung with a full contingent of accessories, takes on a singularly feminine manner. It consists of a silver clip which is attached to a girdle or belt and from which are suspended, by slender silver chains, an assortment of little objects of use to the woman around the house. Châtelaines have been used since the Middle Ages but most in existence today date from about 1740. The appendages of nineteenth century examples in particular are numerous, sometimes undecorated but often quite exquisite. They might include a scent flask, perhaps heart-shaped and delectably engraved, or tapered and part-fluted; an engraved thimble bucket; a pair of scissors in a scissor case, prettily embossed; a decorative needle case; a small pill box; a pencil in a silver sheath with a slip-on lid; or a bodkin in its case, embossed and chased. Keys were often carried in this way but were not always hung from a châtelaine of silver, since other metals or substances – particularly pinchbeck – were commonly employed, and this would more probably have been carried by a person of lesser means.

An *etui* is the name given to a small case employed for carrying various personal items, including those used for needlework. The campaign etui was used by soldiers, in the seventeenth century and later, to contain cutlery, condiment containers, a corkscrew, and other implements.

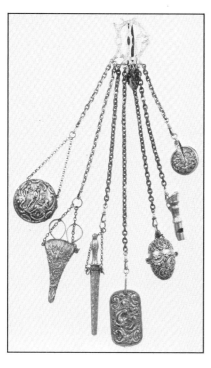

Far left: châtelaine with a pierced and engraved monogram-head hung with seven chains, English or Scottish, *circa* 1870, fitted with a propelling pencil; pin cushion; memorandum case; scissors in a case; 'watch case' box containing a spool, thimble and needle case; egg-shaped case with a spool and pin cushion; and electro-plated whistle. The items are of various late nineteenth century dates.

Left: etui, *circa* 1755, containing scissors, folding right-angle ruler; two spatulas; a snuff spoon; pair of protractors; a knife; and pencil holder.

Skewers

This practical object still survives in sufficient quantity from the late eighteenth century as to be collectable by those who can afford it. Nicely-marked examples are often seen, the hallmarks usually being punched near the loop, and the condition is generally quite good. There is hardly anything very revolutionary about the idea of a skewer, since it has always been the obvious way of holding meat or fowl together when cooking. Originally skewers were fashioned from wood, probably something like dogwood, until the seventeenth century when the hard *lignum vitae* from the West Indies made its appearance. At this stage the refinement of a silver skewer was unknown, a position which remained unchanged until it made its debut in the third decade or so of the eighteenth century.

At this point the skewer was not dissimilar to a bodkin in form, flat of blade and ending in a longish oval grip or loop, which would have been made separately and soldered to the blade. After about 30 years the loop became more ornamental and often incorporated a shell motif in its design, and by the mid-1760s the entire skewer was cast in one piece. With the increase in mass-production methods after about 1770 the skewer was not uncommonly die-struck, and incorporated a contemporary ornamental end near the circular loop in the style of current flatware. Skewers varied in length, depending for which purpose they were intended, the longer examples being about 15 inches in length and used for large joints, and the shorter measuring approximately seven inches, being used for game and poultry or smaller pieces of meat. They were commonly made in sets.

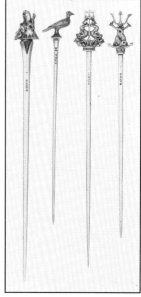

Poultry skewers by C. T. and G. Fox, each with a different cast finial: a boar's head erect; a martlet; and two with dolphins and tridents, London, 1846-49.

Miscellaneous selection
of knife rests in various
materials.

Knife rests

A very interesting collection of knife rests can be built up, particularly if
the collector seeks them in other materials in addition to sterling silver.
The added advantage is that the general cost of establishing such a
collection is lessened. Such a collection can then be sold at a later stage
and the money re-invested in something more costly.

Basically the knife rest is a simple rod with a support at either end which
keeps the rod clear of the table and enables it to support carving
implements. The interest of knife rests lies mainly in the amazing
diversity of ideas, many of which are novel, that brightened up this
ordinary object. Animals were well-favoured as the supports and
included elephants, camels, lions, monkeys, owls and so on. Others may
be delicate, in the form of butterflies, or rather impressive, featuring
peacocks or unicorns. Sometimes the supports are not disguised at all,
perhaps merely decorated a little. Thistles, flowers or gnarled branches
might grace others. Knife rests became more general in the nineteenth
century.

Bookmarkers

Many people do not realise that metal bookmarkers were made, and are
surprised to learn that they exist in sterling silver. Yet they do and, what
is more important, those who wish to collect them will have to apply
themselves to the task quickly for the price of the silver bookmarker is
well on the increase. Bookmarks are shaped something like a blade, the
silver being cut away by about one-sixteenth-of-an-inch in a line running

parallel with the edge of the 'blade', so that this can be attached to a page, with its decorative end protruding as the marker. Handles take various ornamental forms which might include birds, animals, flowers, polished stones, and so on. They mostly date from the later years of the nineteenth century.

Baby rattles

It is a mystery how so many baby rattles are still in existence, considering the rough treatment they must have suffered, but happily this is so and delightful examples can be seen. Silver rattles were known in Tudor times but those available today usually date from the late eighteenth, nineteenth or early twentieth century. Georgian and certain nineteenth century examples were well-made, and incorporated pieces of coral or ivory for gum soothing, little bells and sometimes whistles. They were almost always attractively decorated, perhaps being embossed, engraved or bright-cut, with their bells similarly decorated. They are generally fully-hallmarked, and even the separate pieces might be punched with the lion passant. Edwardian examples also have their attraction, and might be shaped at one end in the form of Punch's head, the handle or gum soother sometimes being made of coral. The types vary and some are quite simple. Look at the bells carefully, as these have often been replaced and thus sometimes do not all match.

Below left: George III rattle incorporating a whistle and teething coral, by Margaret Binley, *circa* 1765.

Below right: Sheffield plate toast rack, late eighteenth century.

Toast racks

These were made in sterling silver and Sheffield plate from the later years of the eighteenth century, and also in electro-plate when this was introduced. Early examples, which were commonly sold in pairs, usually consisted of a tray divided by wire into sections which might contain four, six or eight slices of toast. A frame later replaced the tray and an ever-increasing variety of designs was introduced, including combined toast and egg frames, although it was not until the 1840s that toast racks were registered at the Patent Office, ensuring three years' protection from unscrupulous designers who might steal each other's ideas. Toast racks were decorated in the various ornate styles beloved of the Victorians and, because of this, certain surprisingly simple versions, which were produced in electro-plate and sterling silver during the final years of the nineteenth century and early twentieth, have drawn attention to themselves.

Toasting forks

Toasting forks were made both in sterling silver and Sheffield plate, but the sterling silver examples date from a much earlier time, a rare extant example being made in 1561. A common type made after the last decade or so of the eighteenth century was harpoon-shaped with slightly curved barbs. In use by the turn of the nineteenth century was the toasting fork with a telescopic handle in three or four sections, with a grip often of polished hard wood. Sterling silver examples in the Victoria and Albert Museum, London, include one made in silver and ebony as early as 1669. Other early silver-mounted specimens dating from 1680 to 1735, and a silver telescopic example dated 1805, can be seen at the Museum.

Below left: silver-mounted toasting forks, eighteenth and nineteenth centuries.

Below right: silver-gilt caudle cup and cover, chased and repoussé decorated, London, 1660.

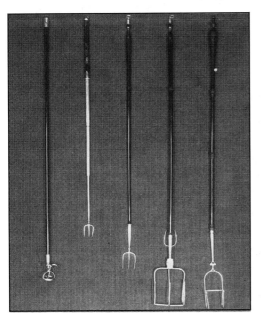

Porringers

This term embraces various forms of two-handled, covered cups which were put to different uses, long-defunct since most of the beverages they contained are no longer imbibed. However, they are attractive vessels and happily still survive in reasonable numbers. Although they are generally described as two-handled cups, they are really more of a deep bowl, with two facing handles and usually a removable lid or cover. The word porringer, it is generally assumed, has nothing to do with porridge, the thought which springs instantly to mind, but is more likely to be derived from the French *potage* (soup), for which it was used.

Another type was the baluster-shaped caudle cup, caudle being a fine gruel mixed with wine, spices, sugar and other ingredients, while the posset cup was used for the drink of that name, which was taken hot and usually made of milk curdled with wine or ale and flavoured with various spices. These vessels were produced in extremes of sizes ranging from those for individual portions – and smaller – to others measuring as much as 15 inches from handle to handle. Some had an accompanying matching salver.

The rounded two-handled cup with a more rotund lower body was commonly decorated by embossing in a floral pattern, while the domed lid or cover was similarly embossed and surmounted by a finial. Some cups are plain or sparsely-decorated. Others have more straight-sided bowls which taper gradually to a foot with a shallow moulded base, and these may be decorated by cut-card work, embossed naturalistic motifs or the delightful chinoiseries typical of the late seventeenth century when these cups were mostly in use. Examples can be seen in the Ashmolean Museum, Oxford, and the Victoria and Albert Museum, London. Sometimes they may also be seen in better antique silver shops.

Porringer and cover, chased and repoussé with acanthus foliage, maker's mark IB with stag, London, 1683.

Glossary

Acanthus The leaves of this plant have been much used in classical architecture in stylised form and appear frequently on English silver, particularly during the neo-classical revival.

Alloy A combination of both base and precious metals, the base metal normally being used to harden the precious metal. Also a combination of ordinary metals, to form alloys such as brass, bronze and so on.

Annealing A method of constantly heating silver then cooling it to prevent it becoming brittle while it is being worked.

Anthemion A pretty motif closely resembling the flower of the honeysuckle.

Applied work Decorative forms applied by solder to the vessel or object.

Arabesque A pattern incorporating scrolls, intermingling foliage and figures in stylised form, derived from Roman murals.

Art Nouveau A style which emerged during the last decade of the nineteenth century and lasted until around 1910. Derived from a combination of Japanese and mediaeval ideas.

Astragal Small and continuous half-round moulding, often combined with other types of ornament such as beading.

Baluster A decorative shape used in stems of vessels, candlesticks and so on. It is elongated and rotund, slender above and bulging below.

Beading Small ornamentation of 'beads', either used by themselves as a decorative border or in conjunction with other ornament such as astragal, bead and reel, etc. Derived from classical architecture.

Bombé A rounded, prominent shape with a low waist.

Boss A rounded knob or stud shape.

Bright-cutting A type of engraving forming a faceted effect, which was particularly popular during the last decade or so of the eighteenth century.

Britannia metal A silvery-looking alloy incorporating tin, antimony and copper.

Britannia standard The higher standard of silver alloy which included more silver (958 fine) than sterling silver (925 fine). This higher standard was compulsory for goods made between 1697 and 1720, after which time its use was optional. Britannia standard silver is marked with the figure of Britannia.

Burnisher A tool with a hard, polished surface used for polishing the silver in its latter stages.

Cartouche A frame or tablet with scroll or rolled-up ends, in which inscriptions, coats-of-arms, initials, etc are inserted. Usually oval, and may also be decorated with other contemporary styles of ornament.

Casting A technique for producing various components and also decoration. A mould of the shape is usually produced, from which an impression is taken in two halves, clamped together, and the molten silver is poured into this.

Chasing Decoration made on the surface of the metal with hammer and punches, but without removing any of the metal.

Chinoiseries Decoration deriving from Chinese ideas, simply used in the final decades or so of the seventeenth century, but becoming more sophisticated during the rococo period and thereafter, when it is often described as being 'in the Chinese style'.

Cut-card work Decorative pieces of silver, cut from a separate sheet of silver – often in foliate designs – and soldered onto the object. Much used by Huguenot craftsmen.

Damascene An inlay of gold and silver beaten into undercut grooves in another metal.

Die-stamping The stamping-out of items from thin silver by means of steel dies.

Egg-and-dart (egg-and-tongue) Ornament comprising alternating egg forms and points.

Electro-plating The application of a coating of silver, using electrolysis, to vessels and objects made of a base metal.

Electrotyping A process for making identical copies of existing objects.

Embossing Producing raised ornament on the outer surface, from the back, with a hammer and punches.

Engraving Cutting lines into the surface of the metal with a sharp tool to remove the metal.

Everted Turned outwards.

Festoons A decoration comprising garlands of fruit or flowers hanging in a curve, which was very popular during the neo-classical revival.

Finial Decorative ornament surmounting the top of a cover.

Flat chasing Low relief surface decoration, without removing the metal, which can be seen slightly from the rear of the article.

Fluting Half-round parallel channels, which may be vertical, oblique or curved.

Gadrooning Inverted fluting used for decorative edges, etc.

German silver A white metal alloy.

Key pattern A repetitive pattern consisting of straight lines intersecting at right angles. Derived from Greek architecture, this pattern was commonly used during the neo-classical revival.

Knop A decorative protuberance on the end of a spoon stem, etc.

Moulding A plain or decorative band applied around an object or vessel.

Niello A black alloy of sulphur, lead, silver and copper, used to fill in engraving to give a contrasting effect.

Ogee A shape or moulding showing in section a double continuous curve, which is concave below passing into convex above.

Ovolo A half-round or curved convex moulding used as a repeat border.

Parcel-gilt An item which has been partially gilded.

Patera A circular ornamentation of classical origin.

Planishing The smoothing-out of imperfections using a special tool for the purpose.

Pyriform Pear-shaped.

Reeding A convex decoration consisting of narrow, parallel ridges.

Repoussé Decorative embossing hammered from the back of the metal.

Rococo An exuberant style which was popular between *circa* 1730 and 1760, composed of shells, scrolls and a wide medley of fantasy, derived from the French *rocaille,* meaning rock-work.

Scorper A small chisel used for engraving.

Sheffield plate Copper to which silver has been fused.

Silver-gilt Silver to which a thin layer of gold has been applied.

Soldering The technique of joining two or more pieces of silver using an alloy that melts at a lower temperature than silver.

Spinning A method of producing hollow vessels on a spinning lathe. A circle of silver is spun around a hard-wood head until it takes the same shape.

Strapwork Ornamental lengths of straight or curved strapping.

Swag A decoration consisting of a festoon of draped cloth.

Thumbpiece A lever for raising a cover, as on a tankard.

Trefoil A decoration consisting of three leaves, derived from the French *trois feuilles.*

Volute An ornamental scroll.

Wire drawing A technique whereby silver rod is drawn through holes of diminishing diameters until fine wire is achieved.

Bibliography

Frederick Bradbury, *Bradbury's Book of Hallmarks* (J. W. Northend Ltd), first edition 1927; revised every year.

Frederick Bradbury, *A History of Old Sheffield Plate* (Macmillan), 1912.

Michael Clayton, *The Collector's Dictionary of the Silver and Gold of Great Britain and North America* (Country Life), 1971.

C. Willett Cunnington and Phillis Cunnington, *A Handbook of English Costume in the 17th Century* (Faber and Faber), 1972.

Elizabeth de Castres, *A Collector's Guide to Tea Silver 1670-1900* (Muller), 1977.

Eric Delieb, *Investing in Silver* (Barrie and Jenkins), 1967.

Eric Delieb, *Silver Boxes* (Barrie and Jenkins), 1968.

J. F. Hayward, *Huguenot Silver in England 1688-1727* (Faber and Faber), 1959.

G. Bernard Hughes, *Antique Sheffield Plate* (Batsford), 1970.

Bernard and Therle Hughes, *Three Centuries of English Domestic Silver 1500-1820* (Lutterworth), 1952.

Charles James Jackson, *English Goldsmiths and their Marks* (Batsford), 1965.

Charles C. Oman, *English Domestic Silver* (A. and C. Black), 1934.

Norman M. Penzer, *The Book of the Wine Label* (White Lion Publishers), 1974.

Robert Rowe, *Adam Silver 1765-1795* (Faber and Faber), 1965.

Gerald Taylor, *Silver* (Penguin), 1956.

G. M. Trevelyan, *English Social History* (Longman), 1944.

Stephen H. Twining, *The House of Twining 1706-1956* (R. Twining and Co Ltd), 1956.

Patricia Wardle, *Victorian Silver and Silver-plate* (Barrie and Jenkins), 1963.

Wynyard R. T. Wilkinson, *A History of Hallmarks* (Queen Anne Press), 1975.

Catalogues and booklets: *White Gold* (British Sugar Bureau); *Touching Gold and Silver, 500 Years of Hallmarks* (The Goldsmiths' Company); *The Colman Collection of Silver Mustard Pots* (Colman Foods Ltd).

Index